PRAISE FOR DAVE BISSONETTE &
*FLIGHT 3407: COMPASSIONATE LEADERSHIP
IN THE FACE OF DISASTER*

"The Clarence Central School District has been fortunate to work directly with David Bissonette on the creation of our school safety plans and emergency drills. David's leadership and expertise have proven to be an invaluable resource to our school district. David has worked extensively with the faculty and staff on preparation and crisis-management strategies, tabletop exercises, and was the lead coordinator for a major active-shooter drill involving numerous emergency agencies. The Clarence School District has been proactive in our approach to crisis management, and Dave Bissonette has served as the leading expert facilitator in that process."

—**GEOFFREY M. HICKS, EDD**
Superintendent of schools, Clarence Central School District

"David Bissonette not only is a sought-after resource within our organization (General Mills Inc.), but he's a very active and passionate safety leader in our local community. I've had the opportunity to see him in action during training situations as well as crisis modes, and I'm always impressed by his knowledge, calming demeanor, and ability to deeply engage stakeholders. He embraces the opportunity to educate others on how to effectively navigate difficult situations, and this book is yet another example of him leveraging his expertise to make a difference."

—**ALLEN BROWN**
Plant manager, General Mills (Buffalo, NY)

"It has been a privilege to have the opportunity to work with David Bissonette over the past several years. I have worked with David as a safety professional for over a decade, and I have called upon his safety knowledge and experience many times.

David has been a featured presenter for several of our safety events in the past. His technical knowledge of his subjects, along with his ability to relate and communicate to the audience, is key to his effectiveness. Dave's technical acumen, easygoing demeanor, and pleasant presentation style engages everyone in the audience.

Technical knowledge of topics, vast relevant experience, effective speaking style, and respect for his audience are the attributes that describe David Bissonette and why I put him at the top of the list of speaking professionals."

—DALE LESINSKI
Vice president of sales, DiVal Safety Equipment, Inc.

"Attending sessions with knowledgeable speakers such as David Bissonette is one way for each of us to stay on top of the important issues faced each day. His enthusiasm, knowledge, and professional manner made the session enjoyable to attend."

—RONALD J. DUNN
Chief of hazardous materials/Homeland Security Bureau, NYS Office of Fire Prevention & Control

"I was fortune to have Dave working for me when I faced my toughest challenge ever as the VP of operations for Perry's Ice Cream. Dave was my safety and environmental manager. Dave led a team of engineers, contractors, and operators to address an odor issue from our wastewater pretreatment plant that had escalated to the attorney general's office. The attorney general was threatening to shut us down if we didn't eliminate the odors that were affecting the neighbors.

Under Dave's leadership, we consulted, designed, built, and implemented a new operation that was up and running before the attorney general had an agreement for me to sign to correct the situation. When I tell people the story, I tell them that what we accomplished was nothing less than the effort put forth by the team that brought back Apollo 13! It was so unbelievable that the environmental engineer the attorney general sent in to accredit the new system said, 'You guys need to write an article on this!' Dave is simply the guy you want by your side when you're dealt a bad hand of cards!"

—BRIAN PERRY
Vice president of operations, Perry's Ice Cream (Akron, NY)

"Dave is a safety professional with an impressive depth of knowledge and experience. Dave has excellent public-speaking skills and does a great job facilitating individual and organizational problem solving."

—TIM TALLEY
Security consultant, Secure Environment Solutions, LLC; commander (retired), NY State Police

"I initially met with Town of Clarence Emergency Coordinator Dave Bissonette at the site less than an hour after the crash, and our coordinated efforts were to manage the incident, but our primary concern for this recovery effort was to preserve the dignity and respect of the victims and their families. Every action that we took over the next month held that concern as our primary responsibility. Dave Bissonette is a team player. He controlled the initial media releases, providing accurate and necessary information to the public, and was completely capable of managing an incident of that magnitude. True leadership qualities are often realized during the worst situations imaginable—pressure under fire—and Dave's leadership attributes became immediately apparent to everyone."

—CHRIS CUMMINGS
Major (retired), New York State Police

"Prepared, knowledgeable, decisive . . . On the night of February 12, 2009, David Bissonette, the Town of Clarence emergency manager, put these leadership skills to the test when Colgan Air Flight 3407 crashed without warning in his quiet suburban community. As I arrived on the scene shortly after the crash, I witnessed Dave's leadership skills in action and his involvement in the organization to the initial response to this tragic incident. He was instrumental in the coordination of the event's ongoing emergency response, as well as assisting long term with helping the community as a whole heal from this tragedy."

—SCOTT R. PATRONIK
Chief of special services, Erie County (NY) Sheriff's Office

"We were so pleased to bring Mr. Bissonette to our fire symposium in Hamburg, Germany, and hear about his personal involvement in the crash of Continental Flight 3407. His experience and practical application was a value to our fire-service professionals."

—VERONIKA TRAUTMAN

Director of training operations, National Fire Academe (Hamburg, Germany)

"I am proud to consider Dave Bissonette my friend and am privileged to have worked with him when I represented the Town of Clarence in elected capacities for a decade and Dave was the town's disaster coordinator. In those ten years, Dave effectively managed the town's disaster response through a hazardous-waste facility explosion in 2002, a weeklong incident as a result of the October Storm 2006, and the loss of loved ones as a result of Flight 3407 in 2009. Dave's compassion, caring, and calm resolve helped set the tone—the bond of relationships strengthened as Dave would daily set forth the five items he wanted to accomplish to make sure the residents of Long Street could move back into their homes and dignity and respect would be shown to the loved ones and families of Flight 3407. Dave's compassionate, selfless, and authentic leadership is a testament to a great person doing great work on behalf of others."

—SCOTT A. BYLEWSKI, ESQ.
Town of Clarence Supervisor, 2009

"David is the consummate professional. He is an excellent presenter who holds an audience's attention and involves them with his presentation. He is an acknowledged leader in the area of emergency response, and his experience is an invaluable asset that he is willing to share with audiences and students."

—STEVEN MACMARTIN

Clinical assistant professor, Medaille College; director, Homeland Security Program at Medaille College

"I have known Dave for nearly twenty years. He has an intrinsic magnetism about him that enhances his natural leadership ability. People are drawn to and look toward such leaders, whether they truly are on the right path or not; Dave is on the right path, as his is one based upon skill, patience, and a studied practiced nature.

Crisis management comes second nature to Dave, and he is truly above all others, as he has dedicated years in perfecting his craft.

Due to his abilities and personality, he is an in-demand, captivating, and extraordinary speaker. While I know him through a professional relationship, his passion for life has endeared him as a friend."

—RICK MANCUSO

Business administrator, Clarence Central School District

"I've been to hundreds of scenes with first responders, and Dave is one of those chiefs who realizes that reporters also have a job to do. He knows that treating reporters with respect and giving us even what little information he can results in the media stepping back and allowing responders to do their job. Flight 3407 struck way too close to home for him, but he struck the perfect balance of professionally conveying information with a very human and compassionate approach. He knows that by talking with media, he controls the message, as opposed to fighting it, and ultimately being disappointed with how it comes out in the news."

—GEORGE RICHERT
News reporter, WIVB TV

FLIGHT 3407

FL✈GHT 3407

COMPASSIONATE LEADERSHIP IN THE FACE OF DISASTER

DAVID M. BISSONETTE

Advantage®

Published by Advantage, Charleston, South Carolina.
Member of Advantage Media Group.

ADVANTAGE is a registered trademark, and the Advantage colophon is a trademark of Advantage Media Group, Inc.

Printed in the United States of America.

ISBN: 978-1-59932-742-6
LCCN: 2016948662

Cover design by Katie Biondo.

This publication is designed to provide accurate and authoritative information in regard to the subject matter covered. It is sold with the understanding that the publisher is not engaged in rendering legal, accounting, or other professional services. If legal advice or other expert assistance is required, the services of a competent professional person should be sought.

Advantage Media Group is proud to be a part of the Tree Neutral® program. Tree Neutral offsets the number of trees consumed in the production and printing of this book by taking proactive steps such as planting trees in direct proportion to the number of trees used to print books. To learn more about Tree Neutral, please visit **www.treeneutral.com.**

TreeNeutral

Advantage Media Group is a publisher of business, self-improvement, and professional development books. We help entrepreneurs, business leaders, and professionals share their Stories, Passion, and Knowledge to help others Learn & Grow. Do you have a manuscript or book idea that you would like us to consider for publishing? Please visit **advantagefamily.com** or call **1.866.775.1696.**

My wife Traci and I respectfully dedicate this book to the victims of Flight 3407 and their families. The tremendous loss of life also brought suffering to our community. But through this tragedy, we have realized the incredible strength and perseverance of the families who have tirelessly worked toward improving aviation safety, helping to ensure that this won't ever happen again to someone else's loved ones. We humbly dedicate this book on their behalf.

As a longtime resident and emergency manager of my town, I was driven and compelled to provide a way of compassionately understanding the incredible emotional and long-lasting effects of such a horrible tragedy. I have trained my entire life in the area of emergency management and am passionate about making a difference when a tragedy occurs. I am committed to making a difference for public safety and for better safety standards.

TABLE OF CONTENTS

FOREWORD

by Nancy G. Light, Clarence, New York

Tragedies and disasters strike when we least expect them. Ordinary days become historical events. Lives are turned upside down in a minute's time. The only hope in those circumstances is that there is someone present who is sufficiently trained to keep a cool head and who knows what to do within the turmoil. If you knew David Bissonette, the Emergency Manager and Disaster Coordinator of the Town of Clarence, you would have to agree that he knew how to manage the monumental circumstances he faced during the minutes, days and weeks after Continental Flight 3407 fell from the sky onto a home in the small town of Clarence Center, New York, on February 12, 2009.

I have known David since he was a student at the Clarence High School where I taught in the 1970's. He was a respectful young man who, at the age of 16, had already become a volunteer fireman with a sincere desire and the drive to become a contributing member of our community. David is just one of those individuals whose life has made all the difference because of the choices he has made. He was never a passive leader; he grew in strength of character and wisdom that would be exactly what was needed in a-once-in-a-lifetime challenge.

David and his wife Traci eventually became our close neighbors and friends. They are a well-matched pair; together they are a team that influences the people around them in a positive way. They are well respected and trusted by those who know them.

On that wintry night in February, my husband Gary and I were in our family room thinking it was about time to retire, when I heard a plane passing directly overhead. It sounded so unusually close that I remarked about it. Within four minutes, I received a call from Traci which changed the peaceful evening to one of grave concern. She said they had just received the call that something terrible had happened on Long Street and promised to keep me informed and updated. We stayed awake all night, especially when we learned it was a commercial plane that had crashed into a home just two miles down the street from our home.

I am so grateful that David had the expertise needed to manage this tragic event, and I am grateful that our town board members had the foresight to appoint him as their official Emergency Manager/ Disaster Coordinator for the Town of Clarence. Every town in every state in every country needs to be prepared to face any dangerous situation that might happen without notice. The content of this book will lead you behind the scenes and will answer the questions you might have about how a group of people involved in a disaster knows what actions must be taken, and in what order, who is the recognized voice of authority in that set of circumstances, and how to cooperate with the media in such a way that facts are reported with respectful sensitivity.

David and Traci have kept the events, stresses, and wounds of what they saw and experienced bound up in their hearts. They are aware that the families of the victims, the volunteers, and we as a community have suffered and been scarred by this tragedy. The reader will find this book a very interesting journey into the center of the scene with an insight into the compassion that David showed the public and our community even in the midst of chaos.

It is not surprising that I thought of David when I read this quote from the occasion in 1910 at which our former President Theodore Roosevelt gave an address entitled "Citizenship in a Republic." To the audience in Paris, France, he expressed his thoughts on citizenship:

> *It is not the critic who counts... The credit belongs to the man who is actually in the arena, whose face is marred by dust and sweat and blood; who strives valiantly, who errs, and comes short again and again, because there is no effort without error and shortcoming; but who does actually strive to do the deeds; who knows the enthusiasms, the great devotions; who spends himself in a worthy cause; who at the best knows in the end the triumph of high achievement.*

(Respectfully Quoted: A Dictionary of Quotations.)

ACKNOWLEDGMENTS

DAVE

To my parents, Richard and Janice Bissonette, who raised me to recognize responsibility and compassion for others in need. It was their influence and the values they instilled in me as I grew up that gave me the foundation by which I lead my life and give to others. I love you, Mom and Dad.

To my first-responder colleagues and friends—every day we work to reduce human suffering and make the community we live in a safer and a better place. We have these common experiences: we have trained together, we have worked large-scale incidents together, we have talked into the night when a tragedy occurs. Our common goal is to help—to reduce life suffering. I am so appreciative of your immediate response when I asked you for help on the night that Flight 3407 went down. It was my lifeline. I can't express the deep gratitude I have for all of you and for the incredible dedication to the work you do every day. With a heart full of appreciation to my brotherhood, I say "Thank you!"

TRACI

I would like to thank my two sisters, Dawn and Darci, for their love and unwavering support through that very difficult time in my life.

They have always stood by me, supporting my decisions and lending their ears. They have respectfully supported Dave in his emergency-management career, listening to the tales of sorrow, sacrifice, and success. I love you both!

I also would like to thank all of my business clients who offered words of encouragement, support, and kindness. It is hard for me to express how deeply moved I am by their words of wisdom and their generosity. It was the simplest of conversations in those days that got me through. Their words lifted my spirit, as I also tried to lift theirs and comfort them with my words. We all were experiencing something that inevitably touched the entire community, and we talked through all of it. I am so thankful and grateful for them all.

DAVE & TRACI

To our extraordinary friends, employees, coworkers, and community members who showed themselves and stood by us through the weeks and months beyond this tragedy. To our entire family who have supported us, stood behind us in the most trying times of our life, and helped to cultivate an environment of love, hope, and well-being. You showed us how to laugh again. We both count all of you as our highest of blessings! All of your prayers kept us going, and we feel so blessed that you are in our lives!

Thank you from the depths of our hearts to those of you who wrote the beautiful letters of encouragement and gratitude and to those who wrote us the personal notes. We'll always treasure those words—and we feel a very deep sense of love, support, and appreciation. You will forever be remembered as special, and we feel you are angels who walked right into our lives and helped lift us out of those dark days. Thank you!

Through the darkness came the light. Our belief in God and in the hopes of a better tomorrow show us that there is light that shines in each one of us and helps us endure and move on even when there are days that seem so dark.

You all will forever be remembered and be a part of our existence. Thank you from the bottom of our hearts.

ABOUT DAVE

Born and raised in Clarence, NY, Dave Bissonette entered the Clarence Volunteer Fire Department in 1978 at age sixteen. He maintained an active status for twenty-seven years, working his way up through the ranks of lieutenant, captain, assistant chief, and hazardous-material (HAZMAT) team leader before attaining the position of fire chief. In 1990, he accepted an appointment as emergency coordinator for the town of Clarence, a position he continues to hold.

During his twenty-six years as emergency coordinator, Dave has been responsible for providing emergency support and guidance on a number of large-scale emergencies, including hazardous material releases, chemical-plant explosions and fires, mass-casualty incidents, regional heavy snowstorms, and long-term power outages.

Also a full-time safety and security manager for a global food manufacturer, Dave draws his expertise for managing difficult disasters from a well-rounded safety career and a lifetime of experience that has led to the establishment of Interactive Safety Services, a consulting firm in 2006. His successful coordination of the crash of Continental Airlines Flight 3407 on February 12, 2009, put his experience and knowledge to the ultimate test. Sadly, the crash tragically took the lives of all forty-nine persons on board and one person on the ground. However, Dave's outstanding work and his dedication to compassionate leadership during the response effort have earned him numerous awards and praise from both the public and emergency-services sectors.

ABOUT TRACI

Married to David for twenty-six years, Traci was born and raised in Williamsville, NY, and has more than thirty years of experience in cosmetology. As a small-business owner, Traci has spent the last two decades of her cosmetology career operating a salon in her hometown. Throughout the aftermath of the 3407 crash, Traci assisted in managing volunteerism, community outreach, and mental-health support for individuals affected by the overwhelming loss, while simultaneously supporting David as he coped with the pressures of a traumatic and challenging leadership task.

INTRODUCTION

At 10:20 p.m. on February 12, 2009, a twin-engine commercial airliner sliced through the wind and rain over Clarence Center, New York, a small, rural town just outside Buffalo. When a pilot error sent the plane hurtling to the ground and into the home of a local family, a late-night phone call to the town emergency coordinator hints at the devastation. By the following evening, the extent of the damage was all but confirmed: all forty-nine passengers and crew on board and one member of the Wielinski family on the ground are dead.

For the next eleven days, emergency responders from Clarence Center and its surrounding townships and counties work to extinguish the walls of flame and investigate the crash site. At the helm of the operation is an unlikely face—a part-time emergency coordinator who has spent nearly three decades overseeing the emergency needs of the town and its residents.

Dave Bissonette has lived his entire life in Clarence. Like his father before him, he had spent most of his youth and young-adult years at the local fire station, serving in roles from junior firefighter to fire chief. At just twenty-eight years of age, Bissonette was selected as the town's emergency coordinator, a position that would put him in charge of decades' worth of paralyzing blizzards, chemical fires, industrial catastrophes, and countless accidents and tragedies. But no other event in his career could have prepared him for the hellish night of fire and rain before him.

With mass casualties and a national spotlight upon him, Bissonette began the unimaginable task of piecing the town he loved back together during its most dire time of need.

In the throes of devastating grief and chaos, Bissonette and his wife, Traci, with a far-reaching community alongside them, remained determined to show the world what ordinary people can achieve when they meet the extraordinary odds against them as one.

This is their story.

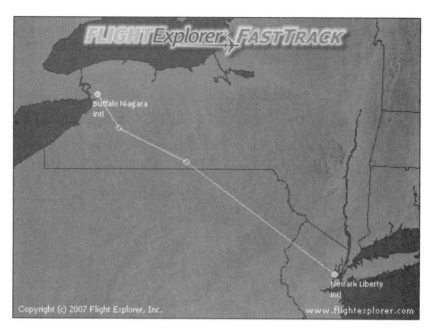

FLIGHT 3407 DEPARTED NEWARK LIBERTY INTERNATIONAL AIRPORT AT 9:20 PM EST

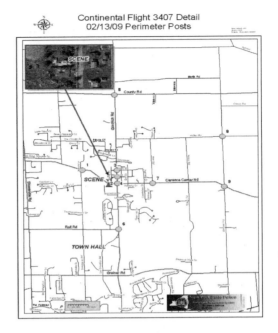

Continental Flight 3407 Detail
02/13/09 Perimeter Posts

BOMBARDIER DASH 8 Q400
OVERALL LENGTH 107 FEET
WING SPAN 93FEET
MAXIMUM SEATING 74
FUEL CAPACITY 5500 LBS (810 GAL.)

C H A P T E R   1

MAYDAY

The weather was miserable. With temperatures hovering just above freezing all day, the snow/rain mix was beginning to turn to ice as the daylight faded. To make matters worse, the wintry mix was inducing localized flooding concerns around Clarence Center, my hometown and primary responsibility as the town's disaster coordinator. The day had been more difficult than most, but it wasn't entirely uncharacteristic either, given the time of year. It was mid-February in northwestern New York, nineteen miles east of Buffalo. Icy conditions were normal for us, but a number of streams and creeks in the area were approaching maximum capacity, and I had to keep my eye on the area flood gauges.

To tend to my civic duties, I had taken the day off from my full-time job as safety and security manager for General Mills. I spent the day working with the highway superintendent, monitoring the water levels, working with residents and property owners, and trying to plan effectively for the possibility of more widespread flooding.

The constant focus for twelve long hours under dismal weather conditions had left me feeling exhausted by nightfall. With threats all week of more rain, I decided to make one more patrol around the area before heading home for the evening. *Maybe I just need to rest*, I thought to myself, feeling exhausted and hungry.

After checking water levels one last time, I drove to a local restaurant to have dinner with my wife. For the past twenty-five years, Traci has owned and operated her business, a hair salon in nearby Williamsville. She continues to work on clients, and this was her longer day. She called me earlier in the day and said she wouldn't be done until after 8:00 p.m. We were both so exhausted that we barely said a word over dinner, a rarity for us, and by nine thirty, we were hurrying to pay our bill and get home.

Only twenty minutes after we had settled on the couch to decompress before bed, my pager went off. Late calls are somewhat common in my profession. You can, and will, be interrupted at any time for a crisis. That's part of the job, and emergency workers accept it. Most first responders go to as many calls as we possibly can. That night, however, I was so exhausted that, at first, I didn't even hear my pager go off.

I was nearly asleep on the couch when it vibrated a second time, but this time Traci heard it and said to me, "David, someone is trying to get ahold of you!" I was just dozing off and wanted nothing to do with whoever was trying to call me. All I wanted was to sleep. I got up with Traci's insistence and went to my phone.

"This is Dave," I said, practically asleep. On the other end of the line was Pat Casilio, a town board member and longtime friend of mine. Pat was a former fire chief in my department, and his experience in the fire service has given him a reliable understanding of what's serious and what's not. When I heard Pat's voice, something felt odd. For him to call me at this hour, I knew it was serious.

"Sounds like we have a downed plane…an airplane crash in town," Pat said. He spoke slowly, calmly—neither of which is uncommon for Pat, an unshakable professional during emergencies. But he sounded distressed, too, like he was distracted by something too disturbing for even him to discuss on the phone. I responded to his report and told him, "I'm on the way."

As soon as I hung up the phone, I literally ran past Traci into our bedroom to change, as she followed nervously behind. "What's going on? What's wrong?" she asked, her concern growing. "Pat tells me there is a plane down just up the street from us, on Long Street."

A plane crash in this area can mean many things. We have some small airports nearby, so my initial thought was that a Piper Cub or a Cessna type of plane experiencing mechanical difficulties must have crashed in Clarence Center before reaching its destination. A call for help when there are likely fatalities or victims in need of rescue energizes you to get up and get going in a way that can't be justly described. Truthfully, I can't recall ever experiencing anything like the feeling I had beginning right then. Shock, worry, urgency, adrenaline, uncertainty—all the strongest emotions were swirling inside me as I moved through the house to put on my coat and boots.

As soon as I was dressed, I took off, heading for the unknown and anticipating something I had probably never seen before. As I drove, headlights cutting through the icy rain, radio chatter began to fill my truck. "We can't confirm the size of the aircraft or how many passengers are on it…" But even with no concrete information about what I was going to find, my heart began beating its way into my head—something was telling me that tonight was going to be one of the longest nights of my career.

As I pulled up to the scene, I saw the nightmare. Flames roared over the tops of trees and houses, illuminating the sleepy neighborhood. Emergency vehicles cast flashes of multicolored lights onto  the surrounding homes and yards, the wintry mix still falling on the buildings and streets. A few residents stood like statues in their front yards, undoubtedly stiffened by the sight, an orange glow rippling across their stunned faces. I knew that a small aircraft could not have generated a fire of this magnitude, so I suspected right then that we were dealing with a commercial airliner of some sort.

When I drove around the corner of Clarence Center and Long Street, I could see that at least one, maybe two, structures were already fully engulfed in flames. I drove to within a few thousand feet of the impact scene and parked, staring in disbelief for a few moments as my worst suspicions materialized right in front of me. *This is not the kind of disaster I have managed before. Oh my God, will I be able to manage this?* I thought to myself, pausing for a moment to take in a breath before opening my door and stepping into the chaos.

As I got out of my truck, I could see that the tail section of the aircraft was the only identifiable piece left. It was the tail section of a commercial aircraft—a Bombardier Dash 8 Q400, to be exact. The regional carrier had a passenger capacity of seventy-four, but we had no idea how many were actually on board or how much fuel remained. What we did know was that the inferno would most likely put up a long and ugly fight. I knew the Clarence Center Fire

8

Department was going to have its hands full. I couldn't believe there could be any survivors from such devastation.

I looked around and saw lots of confusion and excitement everywhere as first responders worked quickly to gear up and contain the area. The residents who had been standing outside for a while were still trying to understand what happened as more began emerging from their homes, mouths opened wide, awed by the horror in their usually quiet neighborhood. Screams and fire whistles sounded all around us as every type of first responder in the area made his or her way to the scene. In Clarence, we don't have our own police force, because of the town's small population, low crime rate, and proximity to larger municipalities. Instead, we have a New York State Police barracks and a sheriff's substation that covers us. Both police agencies already had cars on location. The fire department was already arriving, too, as our firehouse was only about 1,500 feet down the street.

At that moment, we needed to secure the scene and get the public to a safe distance so that we could start putting a plan together. We also needed to understand what happened and what the magnitude was. Because I've spent my entire career in the fire department, I knew what phase one looked like for this kind of incident: put the blue stuff (water) on the red stuff (fire). I looked around, saw that the fire crews were already working to contain the flames as quickly as possible, so my next move was to pull together a few representatives from every group on location. I needed a fire chief. I needed someone to represent law enforcement. I needed airport representation. I needed to pull together what we call a *unified command* and establish an emergency operations center (EOC). In the middle of the mess, I had no idea where this would end up being located—but

I needed to get the people with authority together and start delegating responsibilities.

I started with law enforcement because the fire department really had its hands full. Besides Clarence Center, mutual-aid fire departments from nearby towns and counties were arriving as well. The firefighters needed the latitude and the time to do their job, so I let them work and moved to rally the others.

My job as an emergency coordinator is to have the next step ready. At that time the next steps included gaining control and beginning the investigation, as well as protecting the health and welfare of residents in that neighborhood. To ensure the site's security and residents' safety, I found the state police's leader, Major Chris Cummings—a senior figure in a high-level leadership position within the state police organization. Chris became my best friend right then and there because I knew he was going to be able to mobilize an extensive response from the law-enforcement community. I also knew that he would be critical to securing this horrific scene.

Chris and I got into my vehicle and headed to Clarence's town hall, which I publicized over the fire radio that I would be establishing the EOC at that location. Making this announcement over the radio was a subtle decision—but an important one. Sharing the information in that manner allowed the press, social media, and the public to hear that the leadership of this crash response would not be at the scene anymore. Once that happened, people would all go to the town hall to receive updates and make inquiries, thereby taking some of the burden off the personnel on the fireground. This also helped to reduce the number of unnecessary people who could injure themselves or get in the way of emergency responders.

The victims' families of what was quickly becoming a widely known incident were an immediate concern as well. I felt the most stress over that aspect of the crash—the anguish I knew these families would be experiencing as they made their way to Clarence Center to inquire about their loved ones. Anticipating who was coming was a big part of our functionality at that point because we didn't know who all would end up being involved. We just knew that the whole world was going to be coming within the hour, and it was on us to figure out how this was going to happen, where we were going to set up the rest of our operation, and what kind of infrastructure we were going to need for the incoming agencies to do their jobs. I remember thinking that these initial steps would make or break the effectiveness of the incident's response effort. I had never been so uncomfortable with an unknown before—but then, I had never encountered an unknown with so many potentially disastrous outcomes either. Clearly, the next few hours were going to require a career's worth of experience and self-control.

ESTABLISHING THE EOC

After Chris and I arrived at the town hall, my job was to organize a system that could expand and address all issues related to the incident as they developed. We had a general idea of what we were going to need to address and plan for, but we really didn't have many particulars yet. We wouldn't know the details until we had representatives from each agency in the same room at the same time, and then the challenge would be to keep them together. Depending on your familiarity with emergency-response situations, this can be a surprisingly hard objective to accomplish. This incident was especially difficult, and it had been a big challenge just to get everyone we needed at the EOC to leave the scene. I think we all wrestled with our instincts to remain on the fireground at the time—stalled by the immediate sense of suffering and the flames that continued destroying people's lives and incinerating any hope of a miracle.

Thankfully, representatives from the Buffalo Niagara Airport Operations, the Niagara Frontier Transportation Authority (NFTA), Erie County Emergency Services, a representative fire chief, and some of the town board members, including Supervisor Scott Bylewski, were already moving into the EOC. I had managed to get all of them to the town hall and sitting in the conference room outside the supervisor's office. Most of us knew each other, which was a huge value, and we began making the necessary decisions without much debating. We knew we would have state and federal agencies responding, regardless of whether we called them or not, so preparing for their arrival was a priority. We also needed to know what each department in the room was already working on, who was going to work on what, what the next steps needed to be, what our time frame was, and how we were going to communicate. All these types of small-yet-invaluable clarifications help keep the ball rolling smoothly once more parties become involved and the activity begins to snowball.

Other law-enforcement agencies and fire departments from different jurisdictions were filing in by this point, and the National Transportation Safety Board (NTSB) would be arriving soon as well. Building space, utility support, food and shelter, and all those details were our problems to solve. Knowing my resource limits, I very quickly tasked Erie County Emergency Services with a lot of the operations tasks. I first asked for the use of the Erie County training tower. That's where a lot of Erie County emergency services functions occur, at a training facility about fifteen minutes away from the scene. They have a permanent EOC set up there for large-scale emergencies. We use that facility for all types of county disasters, so I explained my needs bluntly to the commissioner, saying to him, "I'm going to need all of your people and your facility in Cheektowaga to help with this." The commissioner was expecting me to say this, and the request for help gave him the green light to call in his department heads and prepare the academy for incoming agencies.

I then designated our location, the Clarence Town Hall, as the official EOC for ground-zero-type issues. It was where I wanted all security operations, including all the police agencies, to perform their work. The local government would continue to operate out of the town hall, and scene operations would be coordinated from the location as well, simply because of its fairly close proximity to the crash site.

At that time, I knew that there were fatalities, but I didn't know how many. It was still very early in the mission, so I didn't have any good information at that point. I had no idea how many passengers were on the aircraft, and I really didn't know how many injuries or fatalities there were on the ground. For most of us, we were still coming to grips with the gravity of the situation, saying to ourselves, *I can't believe this actually just happened!* And in some ways, I didn't want to know the number of fatalities quite yet. I just couldn't go there. I wanted to focus my thoughts and energy completely on the mission at hand before letting my emotions get involved. Looking back on it, I think I also wanted to keep alive the hope that we would find survivors.

We did, however, have one very important piece of information on hand by then. The mangled pile of burning metal that had fallen from the sky just a short drive away had a name. Colgan Air Flight 3407, operating as a shared regional connection aircraft with Continental Airlines, had departed the Newark Liberty International Airport at 9:18 p.m., bound for the Buffalo Niagara International

Airport with forty-nine passengers and crew on board. Less than five miles out from its destination, the aircraft had fallen from the sky, crashing through a two-story home containing three family members. Two had survived, a mother and daughter who crawled away from the wreckage with minor injuries, while the husband remained unaccounted for.

Guiding my decision making and delegation options was a two fold map, so to speak, in which my experience merged with the protocol for functional processes as dictated by the National Incident Management System (NIMS), particularly the guidelines of the Incident Command Structure (ICS). I have been using this system for my entire career, and it has never failed me. It's a system of delegation, offering a template for creating a chain of command that's vital for every emergency coordinator to know thoroughly. It's also the only way to get a handle on so many things happening simultaneously. I thanked God I was trained extensively in this system because I knew I was going to need every aspect of it.

Proving to be useful in a most-critical time, delegation was happening immediately thanks to our collective experience, longtime professional relationships, and the standardized system for emergency response. I remember seeing everyone get to work with what seemed like supernatural focus and speed, doing what they always do as professionals, but with a purpose and drive that I don't think I'd ever witnessed before that night. All of this occurred within the first hour after the crash. As fast as I was making comments about what steps we needed to take to prepare the EOC, the leaders of these respective agencies were on the phone to start the processes necessary to their responsibilities. I was in awe of what I was witnessing, and it gave me a glimmer of hope that we would get through this. I needed that.

Within minutes we had established communications with the public, which allowed us to have phone lines set up for the public to call in and voice concerns or ask questions. A phone bank was set up in the room next to the EOC to respond to calls. We published a couple of phone numbers to the town hall, and the supervisor's staff pitched in and started fielding phone calls from the public, answering whatever questions they could. Questions or concerns that needed to be addressed further would be passed over to the EOC to be addressed tactically. I remember feeling bad that the staff would be getting difficult questions, such as: "Do you know who was on that flight?" and "Were there any survivors?"

We spent a lot of time the first hour or two determining who the leaders were from the various organizations that needed to be involved and establishing a chain of command and a chain of order to answer questions. These types of meetings don't always go very smoothly. There can be some vacillating between who's in charge and who will work with who and who doesn't want to work on one thing or another because they feel more suited to work on something else. In this case, there was some very quick negotiation and pacifying going on to keep everyone satisfied and confident that they had the right task to do—but overall, it was very professional, with most nodding in agreement or quickly accepting the few compromises that came their way.

Sometime around two o'clock in the morning, Traci arrived at the town hall. She didn't know where I was and knew I wouldn't be answering my cell phone. She had gone to the scene first, and seeing the magnitude of the crash firsthand struck her profoundly. When she couldn't find me there, she thought that I would be at the town hall.

When she finally found me, the extremely emotional ordeal was written all over her face. In fact, I saw something that I don't know I've ever seen in her before that night. For probably the first time in my entire fire-service career, she was scared for me.

Visibly shaken and concerned about what I was doing, she was determined to help. "I'm not going anywhere," she told me. Knowing that I was going to be up to my eyeballs with critical decisions and stress for the foreseeable future pained her, and by the firmness in her voice, I knew this wasn't a negotiable statement. I stared at her for a few seconds, slightly taken aback, and then I said, "Okay. Grab a pen and notebook and stay on my belt loop. I need you to take notes for me. You can be my scribe." I could keep her close to me so she wouldn't have to worry about what was going on and where I was. But I also appreciated the opportunity to put her skills and willingness to help to good use—and we certainly needed all the help we could get at that point. Plus, Traci isn't the type of person to stand around aimlessly in a time of crisis, so I knew that giving her the ability to contribute to the situation was the only option she was going to accept.

She told me something else, too: reporters and production assistants from the likes of Larry King, CNN, and Fox News were calling our home in hopes of getting a comment from me. I knew that the buzz was beginning to reach the entire country, but my greatest public-information concern was about the local population. Literally and figuratively, residents were going to wake up to the knowledge that a horrible plane crash had occurred in their community. They were going to want answers, and I needed to work as fast as possible to gather accurate answers for them. Traci knew it too, and she got straight to work as well, documenting my conversations and keeping a record of what we needed as I communicated orally with other parties on a variety of issues all throughout that night.

I also needed to do some homework before outside agencies began to arrive. An airplane crash was not an incident I had ever role-played or trained to work in or around, even with our fairly close proximity to the airport. For years and years, the common wisdom was that the communities south and west of the airport were the ones that needed to be ready for an airplane crash. Because of the way the runways come and go from the Buffalo International Airport, we had never considered ourselves a high-risk approach hazard for an aircraft disaster. So this type of incident just wasn't on my radar in terms of needing extra skills and training. A plane crash wasn't in my emergency-management plan, either. People ask me for a copy of the emergency-response plan for aircraft disasters we used—and I don't have one. Instead, I had to rely on my prior leadership and training skills. So that was a very intimidating few hours until I figured out who these groups were, what their authority was, and what their mission would be.

What does the NTSB (National Transportation Safety Board) do exactly? I remember asking myself. There's a certain learning curve that goes with every incident, but this one was going to have the NTSB and the FBI transportation regulators, a much larger investigative team, involved in the recovery and investigation. I had never secured a large-scale transportation disaster zone before, so I had never worked with either of these agencies before 3407. I knew that any mass-casualty transportation accident was a role for the NTSB, but I had to figure out the extent of their roles, as well as their protocols, without tipping my hand that I didn't know. And I had to do it quickly. I continued to feel vulnerable and unprepared to interact with these unknown agencies. I remember telling myself to remain calm and that we would work through our issues one at a time.

The problem was that the NTSB is a very independent organization. They don't talk. They don't interact with the other teams. They're almost invisible, in fact. They establish their own private EOC elsewhere and more or less keep to themselves. Their role centered on task-driven objectives that were not the same as mine for the town and its civilians. They simply weren't looking at the same things I was looking at—quality of life, recovery efforts, rebuilding the town, and putting our community back together again. The NTSB's focus revolved around investigating why the airplane came down and why there were fifty fatalities. They needed to search for those answers just like we were searching the scene—but they worked the scene looking for their clues and telltale signs. The difficulty for me was that I didn't immediately understand that they would not be permitted to have any other focus or be involved in any other way aside from determining the root cause of the crash.

Flight 3407 crashed due to pilot error. There were concerns of ice buildup on the wings and windshield, and the incorrect response by the pilot caused the plane's engines to stall, resulting in the crash.

For quite a few days, I was frustrated by this, as I had very little insight as to what the NTSB was planning for the current day, much less the next day. I just had to be prepared to be flexible with their next expectation. You could say that we worked together, but it was more reactive than it was planned.

Another complication was that their objectives were masked by law enforcement's responsibility to support the NTSB. The state police and the FBI were responsible for maintaining the integrity of the scene while the NTSB and the FBI looked for that root cause. That was another layer with which I wasn't familiar—but I had to try to work that into our overall program as the incident developed.

Knowing what I know now, what would I have done differently? I would have had specific conversations with the NTSB's lead investigator to determine what that agency wanted to accomplish and how it was going to interact with the rest of the scene operations. Fortunately, we were flexible and amenable to everyone's mission. So it wouldn't have changed the outcome. However, the stress level would have been much lower if I'd had a better handle on what their next steps were going to be.

As it was, all the unknowns left me in an uneasy situation. So, with no shortage of "next" concerns, I just had to keep going from one to another, expecting that things would fall into place as we solved each problem.

Where are you going with this? I asked myself. Nearly as soon as I asked it, I had my answer: law enforcement. To get some reliable information coming in, I knew that law enforcement would be our best source of communication at the scene. I had a very good working relationship with the New York State Police and the Erie County Sheriff Department, and I also knew some of the FBI agents working the scene. I had enough networking established among these agencies to know that my colleagues on the law-enforcement side had my back, had the town's back, and would keep those communication channels open to the best of their ability.

We agreed to have law enforcement create two security perimeters, one at the scene and a second one about a half a mile away to keep the public a little further back. At sunup, everyone and their brother would be coming to see what happened. We had to be prepared for that, and our officers would also be able to keep us informed with any events happening on the ground. I felt relatively comfortable with that delegation, which is critical in these types of incidents. You have to delegate, and you have to be able to trust the people to whom you delegate tasks to complete them as requested.

The fire department was going to need support, too. Battling a blaze like the one I had witnessed would require hours of exposure to extreme temperatures in gear weighing more than seventy pounds. Word from the scene was that there was still a lot of open flame keeping them back from the impact zone's center, so it was still going to be hours before we could shift gears into investigation and overhaul. In my mind, I was thinking, *They've still got a lot more work to do, which buys me time to continue organizing and solidifying all these next steps.* We still had countless phone calls to make, dozens of people to bring into the fold, and hundreds, if not thousands, of loose ends to address. I knew the fire department would need at least four to six hours more to get the scene under control. However, the crews on point were going to be showing signs of exhaustion and stress soon. I knew that the fire service would be using mutual aid to bring fresh firefighters in as needed.

Next on my mind were the families of our soon-to-be-determined victims. Typical protocol for an aircraft disaster or a transportation disaster has the NTSB sequester the family to protect them from any potentially inaccurate information, particularly about who died and who didn't. Because the NTSB wasn't present until seven or eight o'clock the next morning—and even then there was just a single representative until the rest of their agency arrived—another emergency manager from a neighboring town, whom I had known for many years, took on the role of setting up a center for the families.

All the families had been congregating at the airport, a logical place where you would expect to find information about a particular airplane. We asked them, instead, to go to a location approximately five minutes away from the airport to await further information. As soon as we could confirm details from the scene, the families would be the first to know. This allowed us to protect them, to some degree, from relying on the stream of insensitive information pinging around in the media.

The final step was to continue assessing what we were going to need in the way of logistics, support, and resources. Food for a couple of hundred people, shelter, transportation in and out—those types of things all needed to be decided. Again, aircraft disasters were not something with which I was all that familiar. This was something I really had to be flexible with and move carefully through—listening to others, researching, and learning on the fly about some of the subtleties of this type of incident.

DAY TWO: FRIDAY, FEBRUARY 13, 2009

Day two began with work on the next piece of our immediate-response phase: public awareness and press releases, with all the leaders present.

As the fire crews continued bringing the active danger on scene under control and law enforcement remained in charge of site security, the communications aspect of the operation was quickly becoming my main priority. I knew that many people were hurting immensely and even more were scared and confused, so I wanted to make absolutely certain that they got accurate details as quickly as possible. The last thing I wanted was to have this tragedy worsened because of a poorly run public-information spectacle on my watch. I was sickened by the thought of the town shaking its head, wondering how their lives would be impacted by the tragedy. Worse yet, I feared inflicting even more pain on the families of the victims as they waited anxiously for news about their loved ones.

As the incident commander, I decided to delegate the responsibility of public information officer (PIO) to myself. The incident commander is the person who has ultimate responsibility in coordination tasks. Most commonly, you'll see the supervisor of the town or the mayor address the public when there's a matter concerning public safety. When it's clearly a law-enforcement event, you'll get the police chief. When it's solely a fire-department operation, you'll get the fire chief. But when you have a mixed-agency operation like this one, you need an emergency manager who's there all the way through to the end. This is my town, I live here, and it was important to me that the messages to our residents reflected compassionate leadership.

By that time, we were learning that all of western New York was starving for information. People wanted to know everything they could know and as quickly as possible. That level of public interest remained for the entire duration of the incident, so for two weeks, people were setting their TVs at home to record the news briefs and updates, calling in to the EOC hotline, and flooding the inboxes and social media pages of local agencies with concerns.

Having assigned myself the role of PIO, I was charged with presenting a press release at approximately eight o'clock every morning and then another one at four or five o'clock in the afternoon. That task in itself was a challenge because every time you get in front of the camera, the public is hanging on your every word to understand how far the tragedy extends into the fabric of the community and the lives of the people who were involved. What they really want to know is the residual effect of the incident, both physically and emotionally, and that's an especially sensitive topic to address when there are fatalities involved.

Agencies and their media representatives would also be coming and going based on their tasks (and their tasks' completions) throughout the operation, which meant the public would be seeing a revolving cast of spokespeople without knowing whom they could trust. Because I was the main spokesperson and remained in that position throughout the incident, I very early on became the focal point for the public and the media. That put me in a position I had never experienced before, at least not to this degree, and I had to adapt quickly to the role of being a national face for such a horrible tragedy.

To make matters more nerve-wracking, I had already had a bad experience back in 2006 after a major snowstorm cut through our area, dumping three to four feet of snow on the town of Clarence over the course of a day or two in the middle of October. People refer to it as the "October Storm of 2006." My work in town was not very well received during that response, because communications to the public were poor, and that festered a lot of frustration among the residents in the area at the time. So, in the back of my mind, I was telling myself I had to gain their trust back with regard to communications and not let that happen again. Perhaps that's why I decided in those first couple of hours that I was going to handle all my own public relations on this particular incident—because I wasn't going to let it get screwed up by someone else or another agency.

By midnight, we had about a third of the agencies that would ultimately be needed on hand. The first wave of necessary players that had arrived at the town hall included the airport operations people and different department heads from a variety of offices in the county: emergency services, the county executive, and the town supervisor, as well as the law enforcement, fire service, and local government heads. In all, I had ten to twelve individuals present and working with me when we prepared our first press release. We decided that I was going to facilitate the conversation, with all of these representatives flanking me, and I would give a statement. From there, I would field the questions we had answers to, using the appropriate people around me as a source of information.

I made my first press conference early Friday morning, sometime around 1:00 a.m. We had enough information on hand to tell the media how many passengers were on board, what the plane's flight plan had been, update road closures, and take a few questions. But because we didn't have enough confirmed information to be thorough with every issue, I knew this first press conference was going to be a fairly superficial one. I was going to use the opportunity to acknowledge what had occurred, introduce the representatives around me, and then schedule the next press release for 8:00 a.m. that same morning, when most people would be getting up. But I decided that there was going to be a 4:00 a.m. press conference as well. When I entered the foyer at the town hall where the press had been waiting since midnight, I remember thinking, *I am going to need to take charge of the media before they take charge of me.* There was a lot of emotion and energy, and I determined early on that I wasn't going to elaborate.

Shortly before 4:00 a.m., I had put together a number of talking points for that press conference. We had agreed among agencies what we would be communicating. We then made our way over to the Clarence Library, which is next to the town hall. I walked into the

room and made my way over to a table with microphones sprawled across it. I sat down along with my team and I looked out to see twenty or more cameras take aim at me. I took a deep breath and stood up. The crushing focus from the press was intimidating. I had never felt more vulnerable and exposed then I did at that moment. All I could hear were the sounds of camera's clicking away followed by dozens of reporters shouting questions at me. Even with the chaos reverberating off the library walls and rattling my concentration, it wasn't the media frenzy that made that first conference so difficult. I knew there were people out there who were hanging on every syllable that left my mouth, listening intently for news about their missing loved ones. That pressure was heavy enough to make it feel like my coat had turned to steel. Having something concrete and credible to report was my priority, but I was really upset that I couldn't do more to ease the anxiety I knew the victims' families and friends must be feeling in that moment. I was standing in front of that group to divulge the most up-to-date information we could confirm, but I had to be sensitive with how I said it. Had I known then (rather than finding out years later) that several family members of some of the victims were physically present, I can't be certain that the pressure wouldn't have been too much to bear.

Adding to that pressure was this simple fact in the back of my mind: the credibility of an incident is generated within the first thirty seconds of a press conference. My personal reputation, the reputation of everyone standing around me, and the reputation of everyone involved in the response were at risk. So there was also a lot of *professional* pressure not to stumble or appear ill-equipped in that second conference. The court of public opinion decides your fate within seconds, and you won't be getting a retrial any time soon. With all this pressure, I remember how comforting it was to see my wife in the wings.

I promised myself I was going to speak calmly and carefully and that I would not elaborate outside of my prepared information. I told them exactly what we had confirmed at the time working quickly to get us all out of there and back into the EOC. When I answered my last question, we hurried out of the library and walked back to the town hall. If anyone made a noise on our walk back to the EOC's conference room, it was likely a sigh of relief from our collective chest.

Back at the EOC, we sat at the round table, with everyone immediately engaging their laptops, cell phones, radios, or one another to address issues. At that time we had five department heads present, each with a specific area of responsibility. Major Chris Cummings of the New York State Police was responsible for site security. There were three additional emergency managers at the table. One was responsible for assets and resources; anything coming in that would be of value to the incident—whether it was food, equipment, people, or anything else—went to him. The next was the operations chief;

whatever was functionally and physically happening at ground zero was channeled through him. The next emergency manager was focused on external operations, which included anything happening at the Cheektowaga training tower, coordinating with other agencies that were not on-site and anticipating their next steps. My deputy emergency manager oversaw EOC operations. This was a collaborative group of emergency managers   whom I had known for most of my life—so I knew I could count on them to do their very best.

Next on my agenda was establishing order, a very complicated feat that was weighing heavily on my mind. Again, the term *unified command* is what we use to define an EOC that has a representative from each facet, or each agency, of an operation. I wanted to establish some standardization in the operation so that as more representatives arrived, I would know where to place them within the chain of command, as well as what project for which each would be responsible. This was something that I'd learned from previous experience in the construction industry. When you're building a structure, there's a certain rhythm for the construction process and an order to how and when things happen. One of my stressors concerned getting the right order established so that the response could mature on its own. If things are out of order or if they're not well organized, then the system is always fighting itself and a lot of miscommunication, delay, and frustration ensues.

By seven o'clock in the morning, we were preparing for our third press conference, which was scheduled for 8:00 a.m. At some point I caught a glimpse of my reflection, noting my overnight response attire (i.e., a sweatshirt and pants) from the day before, ruffled hair, and the bags beginning to form beneath my eyes. *You look terrible,* I thought. I decided to rush home and change into my emergency-management uniform before I once again stepped into the national spotlight looking as though I'd just been plucked from a trash pile.

Traci had returned home after that 4:00 a.m. morning press conference to care for our dogs and get some rest. She heard me come into the house, and she rushed toward me just as I was about to leave again, my truck still running in the driveway. "You've got to get a haircut," she said to me, completely serious. I looked at her for a second, brow furrowed, mouth somewhat open. "You've got to be kidding me," I said.

"It will take two seconds," she insisted. "Sit down. I'm giving you a haircut." She was adamant about it and finally was very blunt with me. "I'm so sorry this crash has happened. There's nothing else you can do. The worst has been realized. What's important right now is that you take a breath and relax a minute. So let me do your hair."

I didn't argue, and before I knew it, she spritzed me in the head with water from a spray bottle and proceeded to cut my hair—in about four minutes. I walked out of my kitchen and back into my truck with a fresh haircut and the first chuckle I'd had in what felt like a lifetime. She needed to help, to provide some comfort for me during a time in which she knew I would get very little, and cutting my hair was her way of expressing that. To this day we joke about it, but I really did feel more relaxed as I slipped into my yellow, hi-vis coat and headed back to the town hall for that eight o'clock press conference.

As the media coverage progressed, I more or less became the recognizable face of the incident that the public needed from start to finish. It wasn't until about four or five days in that I realized the world was keying in on my yellow coat. That yellow coat inadvertently became a symbol of the coordinated effort, and I think it helped relieve some of the public's concern too. In some unforeseen way, my appearance indicated to people that the incident was being managed properly. In their eyes, the coat told them that I wasn't someone in a suit and tie trained to speak to reporters. Instead, I was a regular guy with hands-on experience in emergency-response situations, and luckily the public was satisfied with that.

Of course, it can be a good thing or a bad thing to become that public focus. If an incident is going south, with problems and mistakes and people getting upset, you're also that focus. In this particular case, it was a positive thing for me that the public saw me as a constant. People were literally finding comfort in my updates— which became emotional for me later as I was reading the notes and some of the reports that were being circulated. I'm not much of an extrovert, and I certainly don't enjoy being the center of attention, so the fact that I wasn't aware of all the chatter during the incident is a relief to me now. That information didn't come to me until weeks and months later. Looking back, had I known the degree to which the public was focusing on me and how far the story was traveling, the job ahead of me would have likely been even more difficult than it already was.

Ten to twelve hours in, people were starting to see that there was a process, and I was starting to feel like we had the right people in the right places and working on the right problems. Everyone was still pretty overwhelmed, but they were at least starting to see what their purpose was. We began to head toward an order to our immediate containment and security operations, which would ultimately last for the next four days.

Improvised command posts were also beginning to fan out across town to house the growing number of agencies and departments. The state police and the sheriff's department, for example, were now setting up their point of operation in a separate room of the town hall. The emergency services of Erie County were setting up at the Cheektowaga Training Academy, and I knew they would develop their scope from there. Nevertheless, I did not intend to leave the EOC until I was confident that all the assets and agencies were in place and had a direction. If I was going to take a breath and relax, I had to know that every agency had a mission and was focused on putting an action plan together to reach the mission's goal. We also worked to ensure that the resources being offered were being collected, categorized, and documented so we wouldn't lose their value when they were needed later.

By ten o'clock Friday night, I was receiving a lot of peer pressure to get out of the EOC. "Go home," "take a break," "take a shower," "have something to eat in your own house," my colleagues urged, now feeling comfortable in their roles. We were going into the overnight, so I knew there was going to be a lull in operations and progress, as the overnight tends to be a time for planning the tasks of the next business day.

I used what's called a *mutual-aid request* to engage seven other emergency managers from nearby towns to assist in the operation, just in case. I deployed them in all the sensitive areas so they could be my eyes and ears while I was away from the EOC. It was a huge relief for me to know that all of my interests were being watched and managed at all times. In effect, I was allowing myself to be everywhere all at the same time. Once those managers were in place, I decided it would be a good opportunity for me to go home and get some shut-eye. Before I left for the night, I learned the identity of one confirmed fatality. Doug Wielinski, a longtime Clarence Center resident and respected member of the community, had perished in his home, killed when Flight 3407 crashed through his living room.

His wife and daughter had survived, though not even the most experienced of the emergency personnel could understand how.

When I returned home for the night, I struggled to settle down and tune out the event. I kept revisiting the scene in my mind, repeatedly saying to myself, *I can't believe we're going through this.* A certain amount of satisfaction and comfort came from knowing that we were heading in the right direction, but as a fellow resident and human being, I was distraught, still in disbelief over the devastation the accident had caused so many people.

Another thought kept replaying in my head as well: *Can I keep it together? Can I continue the momentum?* I had all kinds of cooperation at the time, but I wondered if it would still be there the next day and the next day after that. Of course, there was no real answer. Only time could determine how those types of questions would be resolved. I was starting to see that this was going to go on for a week or more, and that's a hell of a test for professionalism. To keep all these different moving parts working together would require everyone's very best, even when they were completely drained.

Exhausted physically and emotionally, I concentrated my thoughts on next steps and the confidence I had in my staff, ultimately finding enough relief to close my eyes and fall into a deep sleep. The morning would come early, and the only nightmare to fear was the one happening a few miles away.

CHAPTER 2

LIFE OF EMERGENCIES

My father was a first responder, a fire-police officer, and fire commissioner for the Clarence Fire District. The oldest of his three sons, I can remember playing in his boots as a boy, ready to follow in his footsteps even then. So, when I was sixteen, I joined the fire department's junior-cadet program for youth, which, in today's world, would be an explorer type of program.

I went into the fire service with a handful of friends, six or seven in all, from high school. We all learned firefighting skills and tactics from a variety of senior firemen over the years, many of whom were the fathers of my friends. These men kept us all in a lane as we matured and became more pivotal parts of the fire department organization.

When I reached age twenty-one, I was old enough to be a full-fledged fire department member. There was a strong camaraderie among us, and we all aspired to be chief someday.

Everyone was working through the ranks of being a fireman, a truck officer, and then a captain, climbing the ladder as our fathers before us had. As the group got a little smaller over the years, with people going in different directions, there was still a nucleus of three or four of us who remained. We were there long enough to become assistant fire chiefs, and some of us continued on to become chiefs of the department.

For about ten years, each one of us took our turns in the chair, if you will, to be chief of the department. Dave Baumler, my deputy disaster coordinator for the last fifteen-plus years, was the fire chief prior to me. So we both had a significant background in emergency-management tactics, particularly from the fire-service side of things, even before taking on our current roles. After my time as fire chief, I ran for fire commissioner, a position I'm grateful to have held for two terms.

Simultaneously, in 1990, I had an opportunity to be the emergency-management deputy coordinator for Roy Sheiffla, who was my mentor from an emergency-management perspective. He'd been in that role for twenty-plus years prior to me. It was a very different time then, but the professionalism he had exhibited was always something that intrigued me. He retired within about five years and wanted to pass the reins over to me to continue. As of this writing, I've been in that role for twenty-five years.

So it's been a long history of community service, particularly as a volunteer. The volunteer fire department was obviously a labor of love. The disaster coordinator's job had a stipend attached to it—a part-time salary, really. So while it's a formal position, it's mostly a labor of love.

Community service is only one-half of my career trajectory. Simultaneously, I went to work in the construction industry right out of high school. I started with a local construction company after I graduated and gained a lot of my operational experience there, working my way up in skills from laborer to concrete finisher and eventually becoming a carpenter. I worked for two or three larger commercial construction companies as I progressed, until I eventually became a general superintendent for a medium-sized general contractor. Those twenty or so years in construction afforded me a good, healthy understanding of function and equipment. That's a big piece of my ability to be practical during an emergency from an execution standpoint—what can be done, and what cannot. I credit a lot of that perspective to the construction experience I have

MY LIFE AWAY FROM EMERGENCIES

Traci and I are textbook examples of "when opposites attract." While Traci offers a much deeper and emotional side to our relationship, I tend to be a constant pragmatist. She's very in touch with the human spirit and human needs—personal interaction—and she's very sensitive and intuitive and has crazy love for all animals. So much so that we have two dogs at home, and I get to live there, too. But I love that about her. If I wasn't able to come home to so much warmth and nurturing, I shudder at what my often-stressful life in emergency services would look like.

Traci is also a very driven person; we both are. We don't really take a break very often, which our friends are always encouraging us to do. I have three jobs. She runs a nine-chair hair salon with a staff of talented employees. We have many other interests as well, so we're definitely always on the move. In fact, if it wasn't for our two dogs at home, I'm not sure we would come home at all.

So how do two extremely busy and very different people meet? Well, the answer is as uncommon as our pairing perhaps: from my first marriage. Traci was working at a hair salon at the time, a shop that I and several other firefighters used to frequent. I got my haircut for my first wedding from Traci at that salon. A couple of years later, I was divorced and back in her salon for another haircut. Something came over me, a level of comfort I hadn't experienced around anyone else before, and before I knew it, I had asked her if she wanted to go out sometime. She was less enthusiastic than I was, telling me matter-of-factly, "I don't date clients."

"That's fine," I said. "I'm not going to be a client anymore. Does that change anything?" She laughed at first, but then she paused, eyeing me for a second to see if I was serious. I was, and she finally gave in. "Sure, we can go out for one drink."

That gave us an opportunity to have a conversation and start a friendship, which we maintained for a couple of years. We clicked almost immediately, talking for hours about our families, passions, careers, and everything in between. We grew closer the more we talked, and something about her drew me out of my usual self. She was a firecracker and driven by the things she's passionate about; I love that about her. I'm more conservative and a little more introverted, while she's more of the emotional driver and extroverted one in our relationship.

The two of us offset each other perfectly. She's more of a risk-taker, while I'm obviously a risk-minimizer. She typically goes with her first impressions, and I usually challenge that. But we have always been able to make each other laugh and find our way together. We were married in 1990 and have never looked back.

THE GIRL NEXT DOOR

I (Traci) grew up on Greiner Road between Transit Road and Harris Hill, an area on the fringes of Clarence and Williamsville. It was rural and known for its farm fields more than anything else. I spent most of my time as a kid playing outside and loving every minute of it.

Even though I technically lived in Clarence, I went to Williamsville East High school because my father was a teacher in that school. I became extremely interested in cosmetology during my junior and senior years in high school, attending the BOCES (Board of Cooperative Educational Services) Harkness Center, a trade school, to study cosmetology. After I graduated, however, my father wanted me to go to Buffalo State College, where he had gone, to get a teaching degree. "Just in case you cut off your hands and can't do hair anymore," he joked. I listened to my father's advice and went to college—for eight weeks—before I found myself sitting in the parking lot crying over the phone to him,

"I hate it here Dad. I just want to cut hair."

"Okay," he said. "At least you tried. You know for sure?"

"I'm sure," I said. "I don't like college at all. It's not for me."

After my short college experience I worked two jobs simultaneously, bartending and hairstyling. I worked hard to gain clientele and build a business that could support me. At this one particular salon I was working at I built up quite a following of firemen and their wives. But this one man in particular everyone seemed to really like; his name was Dave.

He was friendly and polite and he was getting married to a girl whose hair I was going to put up for their wedding. It's funny now when I think back as I was excited to style her hair and their entire wedding party! After several years of not seeing either of the two, I said to one of the fireman's wives, "Wow, what's going on with them? I haven't seen them in a long time." She said, "Traci, they're getting divorced, and I think you should be dating Dave because I think you guys would be a great couple."

I was shocked at first. "What?" I said, confused and embarrassed. "No, come on, you're joking."

"Yup, you and Dave. I think you guys would be a great couple."

I said, "No way. I don't date clients. I never will."

Then one day he came into the salon with his roommate—I was surprised to see his name in the book, but I was also happy that he came back. I sat him down, and he said to me, "I think I'm losing my hair. Is it looking less to you?" I tried not to laugh and ran my fingers through his hair. "Oh no, it looks fine." I didn't have the heart to tell him that he was definitely developing a bald spot.

The girls who worked with me would say, "That Dave, he is such a nice guy, don't you think?" I said, "Yes, he is. He has a great smile, and he's kind of cute too."

So when he asked me out some time later, I agreed. We talked about what was going on in his life and about his passion for the fire hall. It was only then that I realized he was from Clarence and had grown up very close to me. I was asked out a lot, but he was the only client I ever dated, and then I married him. Crazy, huh? It's worked out better than either of us ever could have ever imagined. We are so perfect together, and I consider him my best friend. As hard as it is for me to believe, we have been married for twenty-six years. It only feels like it's been a couple of years. I am so blessed, thankful, and grateful that David is my husband. If I had to do it all over, I would choose him again!

PRESENT-DAY CLARENCE

I (Dave) would characterize the town of Clarence as a second-ring suburb to the city of Buffalo. It's population hovers around thirty thousand, encompassing approximately twenty-eight square miles. The town is not a heavy-industry suburb, but its population has been steadily growing for the last twenty-five or thirty years because of its reputation as a good town to raise a family while working elsewhere in the region.

That population growth has accounted for Clarence's diverse working-, middle-, and upper-class income levels. We have truly exorbitant and high-end subdivisions where homes average $1 million to $3 million, and then we have homesteads and farms that have been in families for four and five generations. We have the full gamut of residential tenure here.

Without a police force of its own, Clarence is serviced by a state police barracks and an Erie County Sheriff substation. It's also serviced by six volunteer fire departments and a contract ambulance service. It has its own school district, comprising a high school, a middle school, and four elementary schools. And, more relative to our discussion, it has one of the best-trained volunteer fire services in the area. The departments pride themselves on bona fide credentials, both on the county and state level, so training is a constant. Thankfully, the communities in this area are fairly well-to-do, so there's a solid tax base to keep the fire departments well-funded.

Traci and I were both born and raised in Clarence. Perhaps being lifelong residents of Clarence has given us a deeper sense of responsibility to the community than we likely would have felt had we just moved to the area. But the residents of Clarence, overall, have always taken a lot of pride in their community and level of involvement. Clarence has always been dubbed one of the more affluent suburbs in this region. It started out as a farm town and became a well-to-do suburb, yet still maintaining its hometown feel.

The town has done a good job keeping the cozy, small-town aspect of Clarence intact throughout its growth as well. We've had moratoriums on new construction on and off over the past thirty years, which has really kept growth to a slow and careful crawl. One of the reasons Traci and I still live here is because Clarence is still a tight-knit community, one with a history of residents working together, across all social lines, to improve our collective neighborhood.

That same support structure revealed itself in spectacular fashion over the course of a tragic two weeks following the crash, with what felt like the whole world watching.

CHAPTER 3

ON-SCENE: PLANNING IN MOTION

DAY THREE: SATURDAY, FEBRUARY 14, 2009

After more than twenty-six hours of nonstop activity, I had expected to go out like a light Friday night, crashing onto the bed fully clothed and snoring before my head even touched the pillow. Instead, I struggled to unplug from the incident and wrestled myself to sleep for more than an hour. Images of the scene flashed across my eyelids most of the night, the conflagration that was going on there, and all of the shocked chaos that echoed in my mind. I was up again at half past six in the morning, so anxious to see what had transpired overnight.

The next press conference was, again, at 8:00 a.m., an event that would begin my day for the next several days. I dressed and headed back to the town hall, rehearsing a summary of the past twelve to eighteen hours and of what we would be doing for the next eight to twelve. I also needed to have the appropriate panel of agency representatives prepped and briefed, so we wouldn't embarrass each other by drifting out of our lanes. I was very firm about not elaborating, so we ensured that the agencies had a panel representative to answer questions related to their roles. So, for example, during those first couple of days, we had, in addition to myself, a representative from the state police, the NTSB, the township, the FBI, and the sheriff's department. Because it was more about a command-and-control situation at the time, we didn't need any more voices than those.

We would have a briefing before every press conference, with each panel member agreeing to report on two, maybe three, bullet points. I would facilitate the conversation with reporters and answer all the questions that I could before deferring to the appropriate representative. For instance, questions and updates on the investigations I would defer to the NTSB. Questions about curfews and access to the area I would defer to the state police. There were several questions from the public about how they would pay their taxes, as they happened to be due at the time. I deferred those questions to the town supervisor. Everyone had a role at the table and needed to be prepared. My urgency that morning was to get to the town hall and address that preparation together so we could maintain credibility and pass on good information.

We were successful, I believe, in achieving that goal, and the press conferences became easier and easier as we found our rhythm together. That kind of camaraderie began appearing in other ways, too, revealing to me just how deep and far-reaching the kinship among emergency-service members really was. I spent thirty years developing my relationships with all these agencies as a fireman and fire chief, but to see all those years come to fruition in a single incident is moving to me even now.

That bond showed itself in ways large and small. It came from a gesture or handshake, a word or phrase, or in unspoken ways—and we moved through the mission much more efficiently as a result. I began to see this network all around me. The state police major, the Buffalo fire commissioner, county and state first-response agencies and professionals—we all knew one another by name. That kind of thing was priceless. There was no need for introduction or formalities. "My name is _____. I'm with _____ department, and I'm here to help with _____." All of that was eliminated, replaced instead with quick-fire exchanges. When I saw a department head, I could say, "Hey, Chris, good to see you. We've got a mess here. We need to go right to work." And his reply would be just as direct. "Okay, Dave, what do you need?" That's how I got moving so quickly in establishing my organization, and that's really what helped us move through the entire incident so rapidly.

Those relationships proved particularly helpful as federal agencies and private investigators began pouring into the scene. With more than forty-three different agencies involved from front to back, we needed an order to delegate tasks, and those personal relationships were certainly an asset to establishing order! While the NTSB operated separately, the NIMS command framework allowed us to integrate the other forty-two-plus agencies into the ICS, which was a centerpiece of what we were using to ramp up and ramp down the incident from a management perspective.

It's fairly well known that the working relationship between a federal agency and a small-town community tends to start off with a superiority complex. As they say, we only get one chance to make a first impression, and fortunately for us, we had our act together and prided ourselves on creating a fair and equitable delegation of tasks in our EOC.

Later that morning, I boarded my first aerial survey of the scene, flying a few hundred feet above the smoldering char and still-burning wreckage as crews worked tirelessly to extinguish the last of the inferno. The perspective was important for me. I needed to get a feel for the incident and know that it was manageable, to see that this was something we could handle. As we circled the crash site, I knew what kind of work was ahead just in that little patch of ground in this neighborhood. I was still coping with the number of human lives lost—but for the first time since I laid eyes on the incident, I felt confident. Seeing the choreography of our fire departments and law enforcement from above, I knew we were prepared for the challenge on the ground. Getting the political and operational leaders back at the EOC to choreograph in the same way would be a much more delicate task.

LEADING LEADERSHIP

The incident command structure (ICS) is all about recognizing one's personal limitations. Because everyone has a limit, we tried to limit each other to no more than five primary tasks. For instance, I retained five or six tasks during this incident, and every other subject had to be assumed by someone else. Designating people as chief of operations or chief of communications, for example, and getting other people to be accountable for other subjects was a priority. It wasn't perfect, of course, but we all recognized the structure and expected to be delegated tasks from the command system that we had established. That gave us an automatic start-up point, in that people were expecting delegation and knew their roles were to carry out the tasks assigned to them. With a minimal debating, we could quickly move to address problems as they arose—something that gave us an incredible advantage with regard to our efficiency during the operation.

On the other side of that coin, these federal agencies and other teams from outside the local network never know what they're going to get involved in either. If an NTSB agent rolls into suburbia—Clarence, for instance—they don't know me from Adam until we have a conversation and he or she sees what our operation looks like. Sometimes agents have nothing to work with, and sometimes they arrive to find a town with a very well-oiled machine already in progress. That makes their jobs much simpler, as they can focus on their tasks rather than first building an entire infrastructure in which to work. For this incident, they had very solid organizations already established here with the state police and the FBI's Buffalo office. We had our act together, so they were able to come to town with an infrastructure already in place and hit the ground running with tactical and task-oriented objectives. That allowed for better cooperation from other agencies, and the reason was simple: when people respect the command structure, they're more willing to follow its commands.

Around this time, my partner, Dave Baumler, and I also had to begin dealing with our professions outside the mission at hand. Dave and I both have full-time jobs, so anytime you work on a large-scale disaster that takes days and weeks to coordinate (like 3407), you hope to have your full-time job when you come back.

I was fortunate enough to be working for a global company, General Mills, and they couldn't say enough positive things or do enough to help support my efforts. Dave, on the other hand, was working for a smaller company and had to go back to work after three days because they needed him. Losing Dave not only left me shorthanded but also missing a key collaborator whom I had known and worked with most of my life. Had I not had so many others rushing to Clarence to assist, Dave's absence would have left a huge void in terms of morale and workflow.

Luckily, we were starting to see more consistency in our planning. The county had gotten its operations center up and running. The NTSB had its own command post at a hotel in the next town over, as well as its own on-scene command post, supported and operated by the FBI. So NTSB really was separate and apart from everything else, a tactic it practices to maintain its individuality and independence. I continued counting on my counterparts in the state police to keep me in the loop with regard to what the NTSB was working on next, as NTSB representatives still came to very few planning meetings, even days into the incident. Every day we met to discuss what had been accomplished and what the next steps were, but they came to very few of those. Instead, we used the intel from our state police partners to plan around what the NTSB was going to be working on next.

The emergency operations center at the town hall, on the other hand, was now occupied by multiple agencies and their representatives. To keep order, we were still following the unified command model we had established in those first twenty-four hours. We were starting to get organized and find a groove, even with the added agencies and faces around the room, and that felt really good. I was working with a large team of skilled and competent individuals, and the pressure I had felt early on was beginning to subside somewhat. Saturday morning's press release was also important in helping the public understand what had transpired over the past couple of days, where matters stood at present, what progress had been made, and what next steps they could anticipate—which alleviated a lot of the worry and confusion around town.

DAY THREE: AFTERNOON

The fire department had successfully extinguished the fire and fully stabilized the scene by Saturday afternoon, so at that point we began reorganizing for the investigation and remediation phase of the operation. We needed to dismantle and sort the entire scene, one piece at a time. We knew this was going to be a huge next step, and we anticipated three to four days to go through the wreckage and categorize every piece of debris that was on the site. Fortunately, the county, state, and federal governments were all present and bringing their expertise and responsibilities to the incident.

Their presence allowed me to take a breath, focus on tactics, and start looking for trouble spots in our plan, which was a lot of my responsibility: keeping a high-level overview on all the moving parts. This included visiting areas of the operation personally to assess the progress. I kept going back and forth to the county training center and walking through the operation there, checking in with various agencies and disciplines, talking to the county executives, talking to state emergency-management representatives, and then heading back to the Clarence Town Hall to record my findings.

At this point, there were really two phases occurring simultaneously: victim recovery and root-cause investigation. So as we worked the impact zone, federal investigators looked for a mechanical root cause while medical examiners (MEs) were right next to them recovering remains, personal effects, and things of that nature. The NTSB was in charge of all things related to the debris because a lot of it was going to a third site to be reexamined by investigators.

The MEs and the NTSB have to work right next to one another so that when one thing is uncovered, the other agency is right there to fulfill its role. It makes for a very compact incident regardless of the size of the scene, and we obviously were not walking acres and acres of mountainside looking for evidence. Everything was on a single piece of property measuring 250 by 375 feet. I can't stress enough how compact our scene was—and yet everyone managed to keep off each other's toes, literally and figuratively.

The entire incident—not just in this phase, but from front to back—was structured on *next steps*. As one agency finished its job, the agency responsible for the next one took the lead. When going into the investigation and remediation phase of an incident like ours, the lead is the NTSB and the ME's office. Every other agency's role is all about supporting those two agencies relative to their tasks.

For instance, it was still hanging right around the freezing mark in Clarence at the time our second phase of operations kicked off. We used a lot of water to fight the fire that was freezing on the surface and needed heaters adequate to thaw the ground. Those requests went back to the command post, and our resource officer there located heaters to bring out to the scene so our progress didn't stall. Lighting, containers for debris, protective equipment, tools—all of these types of resource needs are based on a task that's being executed to make that task successful. Those needs became our main purpose at that given point.

So, in the field, we had what I call "huddles" every few hours. Individuals from each agency came together to talk about their progress or their lack of progress and what we needed to do differently. That information was then relayed back to the EOC for support. So if we needed more people here or different equipment there—whatever was needed to make the task successful, that was the mission.

TENSIONS FROM WITHIN

Things were running smoothly from a resource perspective—but maybe not as smoothly from a personal and psychological perspective. Moving into days three and four of a very high-stress environment, not everyone was getting their way or meeting on the same page. Our operation certainly wasn't perfect, and we did have some frustrations boil up on the scene as a result. As was to be expected, we also had leadership tensions arise among emergency management, law enforcement, and local government. We kept our tiffs to ourselves and worked to resolve each one as it surfaced, determined to keep the operation professional and centered on the task at hand, as well as the larger implications the mission represented. That being said, we didn't have anyone leaving the scene in a huff or taking his toys and going home. We worked through our problems, so as not to disrespect the human tragedy that had occurred. There was a mutual understanding that this job wasn't going to go away, and we all needed to stay focused and work together toward a common goal, which at this point was to get the scene cleaned up collectively and the community returned to normal as soon as possible.

When problems between two individuals or agencies did arise, they usually occurred as we were finding or refining our hierarchical rhythm together. Two people might be volleying for who would take charge of a particular subject, for instance, and a debate would ensue. "Why isn't it me? You know I have a responsibility to this subject. I should be in charge of that one."

Some of this was driven by ego, but a lot of it was simple logistics and confusions over roles due to agencies or individuals that had never worked in tandem before this incident. To resolve these conflicts, the first step was to recognize the problem and assess the arguments each party was making. Next, I would address it with the parties involved, either directly or indirectly through their superiors, and if we still couldn't get it resolved, then a player change had to be made. Otherwise, the damage to the operation would have become an operational challenge, and I couldn't let that happen.

A good example of some of those tensions occurred within our own fire departments. Why? Territorialism and pride inflated by the emotional nature of this hometown tragedy is the short answer. Flight 3407 had fallen in the Clarence Center fire district, which meant that the Clarence Center Fire Department was the lead fire department in charge. I had served my career with the Clarence fire district, which was the next district over on Main Street.

I understood those feelings, but I had an obligation to serve the bigger picture. I engaged in a conversation with the Clarence Center fire chief, Chief David Case, a longtime friend, and explained to him that because the fire was out, his company had completed its mission and could now pick up and put itself back in service. A different group would begin the recovery phase, and that should not be the fire department's job. He didn't agree with me, and his command staff began to challenge my authority, "Dave, this is our fire. This is our disaster. This is our incident." It took me a couple of days and some other people intervening to help me get across to the fire chief that, one, this wasn't their job anymore, and two, they really didn't want to be a part of the next phase, which was going to be recovery of remains and the deceased. While that's not the task of the fire department, this was a very emotional incident, and his fire company was dead set against letting anyone else come in and pick up where they left off. They felt like they needed to finish the job all the way to the end, and while that's admirable, it just wasn't realistic.

We were also working under a state of emergency, which gave me complete authority to do what I needed to do. It was my job to get them to realize and accept what was best for the incident, and while it might not have been what the firefighters of that particular department liked, I had to find the best solution for the overall incident. In this case, that meant looking out for the residents in the town of Clarence, as well as the first responders.

Obviously, we always want to come to a peaceful resolution when tensions mount, and we all understood that everyone was hurting, particularly the firemen who were first on location and perhaps felt the most pain, as they traditionally deal with the living.

That's also part of my role as a public servant and disaster coordinator working under the authority of the town's supervisor. New York State, in particular, is what's called a *home rule state*. When you go into a state of emergency, the disaster coordinator or the supervisor of that town has final authority on all matters. No one wants to go there, but the buck does stop with the disaster coordinator and the smallest political entity.

A good friend of mine tells a story about two construction laborers, both digging holes. One laborer is told to dig a hole six feet by six feet and to have it done by noon. The other laborer is told the same thing, except that his hole will be filled with concrete and later serve as the foundation of a bridge. Now, one laborer is a ditch digger and the other is a bridge builder. Who do you think respects the process more? My money is on the second laborer who understands his purpose and the reason for his effort.

For emergency managers, it's important that we not continuously gauge someone's need to be there. Everyone has a mission, so if we make clear that we recognize their purpose and that every mission is going to be satisfied, then more often than not the agencies will settle down. Once they do, we can focus on a reasonable chain of events so everyone gets what they need in a timely fashion.

There's a leadership opportunity in these moments, as well, to manage priorities and have a conversation that generates good cooperation. That's a key success factor! In most situations, we can keep everyone working on what they want—but there has to be order and coordination to avoid confusion and the chaos that trails it. That's what a unified command structure is all about: keeping all your assets close so things don't go off in the wrong direction and damage the situation.

As for Chief Case, he and I are still good friends. His was a reasonable mind to talk to. The general feeling was that this was their fire—their blood, sweat, and tears—and they should be there until the end because of that fact. Understandably, there was a lot of emotion and pride in being there, which compounded the feeling that they were owed the opportunity to be involved if they wanted to be. I probably would have felt the same way myself if I had been suited up and on the ground from day one. Luckily, Chief Case and I understood each other's position, and our mutual respect for each another and our respective roles allowed us to smooth the ruffling feathers without causing the operation or our friendship any harm.

THE MISSION OF MOURNING

The town board was also standing by as a resource agency and took on various minor roles, such as coordinating volunteers and donations and working with the memorial side of the tragedy. That was a whole task in itself—respecting the mourning that was happening among both the family members of the deceased and the local community.

To ensure that aspect of the incident was handled responsibly and with dignity, the town board would take on small roles where they felt comfortable. The town supervisor was with me for every news update and press conference, receiving a couple of minutes each time to key in on a few bullet points that he felt were important.

The town's business was still being conducted, as well. Even though we had this disaster to help remedy, the supervisor still had to make sure that the town's business was being addressed and the quality of life was being maintained. My job was to keep moving around the active areas of the incident and checking in, observing the operations so I had a firsthand feel for what was going on or not going on.

There's a certain amount of professionalism needed from the person running the show to stay in touch. So when I was at the Erie County Training Academy or on the scene, I walked through the area and said thank you to a lot of the first responders, had short conversations with the leaders, and was involved in their tasks before getting back to the town hall. As incident commander, I didn't want to lose touch with the issues of the hour or the day. That meant that my job on the ground was to ask, "Is there anything you need? What's not going well, and what can we do about it?"

All of the personnel working during those days had a solid purpose, which I think is extremely important to any mission. It's human nature that when a person feels valued, the work exceeds expectation. So morale was a priority, and everywhere I went, it was high. Obviously, there was a lot of sadness. We were working on a mass-casualty event in which fifty people had lost their lives, after all, and that was certainly weighing on everyone's minds every hour of every day. But having a purpose and a resolve carries a lot of people through a difficult time. There was no casual attitude about that. We all took our jobs very seriously, remained focused and determined, and because of that collective mind-set, I believe we got the highest level of professionalism and respect out of every single person involved in the response.

FIRST STEPS OF DISASTER RESPONSE

- **Isolate, Contain, Reduce, Secure**: Our first step was to let the fire departments and law enforcement handle their tactical missions of isolating and containing the active danger, reducing vulnerability, and securing the scene to protect the public.

- **Assess Public Needs**: Our second step was to make sure displaced residents were properly cared for and sheltered. In this case, most of the affected residents were finding help from friends and family, and we didn't have to open any shelters.

- **Public Awareness and Media Communication**: Consistent press releases with accurate information are vital to keeping some control over media depictions and public order around your scene.

CHAPTER 4

A LIGHT OVER DARKNESS

I believe the spirit exuded by our first responders rippled out into the community as well. While the mission for everyone on the scene was clear and firm, outside the immediate incident area, the public was so close—but could not really be involved. The pain that the community was feeling—the depression, the helplessness of not being involved but being right there—that was a condition that needed to be addressed. In fact, it's a condition that must be addressed in any large-scale tragedy sooner rather than later.

To help with that aspect of the disaster, we used memorials as a place for people to go and show their feelings, offering their sympathies and respect for the lives lost. This was probably more of a psychological impact, and it's importance can't be measured with words.

Within the first few days following the accident, we arranged for the victims' families, a few hundred people, to be taken by bus down to the scene. Traci and I were having lunch at the local corner coffee shop when three white, unmarked buses went slowly by. Traci saw this and stopped talking in midsentence, realizing what was happening. She choked up immediately and didn't speak for a while. We both prayed for the families and what they were going to see. That was a very emotional and difficult moment for both of us.

Once the families arrived, everyone was given an opportunity to reflect and leave items at the memorial they had erected at the site. All the families were able to bring flowers to the scene, and they put them in a centrally located spot so they could stand, pay their respects, and feel the location, if you will—simply to experience the environment where their lost ones came to rest. Two days later, we moved the entire memorial out of the hot zone to a local church's front yard. The church erected a tent over it, and people from all over could come and leave their offerings at what was becoming a larger memorial of flowers and personal effects. Traci and I later visited the memorial to pay our respects.

People wanted to have a purpose, and they wanted the victims and their families to feel valued. Everyone seemed to want to do something, and that inspired all of us working the scene. If an emergency-management team doesn't recognize the nature of grieving and how to help people heal while the operation continues, that—in my opinion—typically turns into frustration and negative energy toward your incident. You need to task people specifically to help coordinate community involvement so the residents can be present and active in the incident. After all, it is happening in their town, right in their backyard, even. If you're so fixed on the tactical piece (which is no small task, mind you) that you don't make room for mental health and community morale, then the whole operation feels it and begins to suffer.

We talk about first responders and the critical stress debriefings we receive, but the same exposure is occurring within the close fringes of the community. How are we going to help them cope with a tragic situation that has just occurred in their backyard? Well, in addition to letting them express themselves through memorials, we encourage them to volunteer in various secondary aspects where a nonskilled person can have a value-added function.

There were plenty of examples of this around 3407, but one that I remember particularly well was what I call the "Cookie Brigade." These were three young boys who took baskets of cookies to the fire hall where first responders were taking a break. These young men would walk around the banquet hall with cookies, because who doesn't feel better eating a cookie? They were as cute as a button, and you could not keep from smiling as they walked from table to table handing out cookies. We all smiled and thought, *How awesome is that?* Those three boys had no idea the value they brought above and beyond the cookies.

There are limits to how effective this type of community involvement can be, however, and incident commanders have to stay vigilant when deciding what level of involvement is productive—and what may prove to be unproductive. When a woman asked to visit the scene with therapy dogs, for instance, my instincts told me this was a request that may be reaching too far. These were dogs that went to hospitals or visited people who were ill and in need of a pick-me-up, and I questioned how they would behave on a major crash scene like ours. But the owner insisted, promising that if she could take her dogs down to the scene, it would be a morale booster for the first responders working the scene. I remained hesitant because it was not a controlled environment and certainly not a place for dogs, albeit trained dogs that were supposed to be able to handle difficult environments.

Traci knew the woman and she told me, "Go ahead, try it." I eventually approved her to take three of these therapy dogs down to the scene as long as I went with her. However, we didn't get more than a couple of hundred feet past the security line when the dogs started acting strangely. There were all kinds of scents and activity that the dogs couldn't ignore, unfortunately, and they were just completely ineffective as a result. The owner immediately turned around and said, "This isn't for us. We need to go, but thank you for letting us try."

With a no-rescue incident like 3407, the dynamic changes. People have to come to accept that what has happened is a tragedy across the board, and that may lead to a greater need to show one form of compassion or another to the families and to the overall sadness of it all. For us, the only thing we could do was minimize the agony of the living, the victims' friends and surviving relatives, and the community. That was all we really could do, unfortunately—and that became painfully apparent to me the moment I realized that even therapy dogs couldn't alleviate the trauma.

COMMUNITY IN CRISIS—TRACI'S STORY

One of my clients and some of her friends had gotten together in the days and the weeks after this crash to make black-and-white memorial ribbons for everyone in town to wear. They wanted to recognize the families and show their support, so they made hundreds of these ribbons for people to pin on their clothes. They also had ribbons that they tied around the trees throughout our town. Within days, there were black-and-white symbols for the victims all over town.

There were yellow ribbons around the trees for the firefighters, too, to recognize how hard they were working to resolve the crash. Right up the street from our home, at one of the churches, a memorial site of flowers, balloons, teddy bears, and other mementos grew by the hour.

Out of the darkness comes light, I've always believed, and these people were living proof of that. They were bringing their love and their light to a very sad time in the middle of winter the best they could with whatever they had. We were starting to feel the effects of that, too—but there was definitely a huge heaviness still resting upon our shoulders. It felt like lead weight for Dave and I probably more than most other residents because of the gravity of his efforts to coordinate the relief response, as well as what we were feeling after witnessing the scene so many times.

But those sparks, those rays of light brought by others through this town, felt really good and helped lift our spirits. All we could do was pray for the victims and their families. We sent healing prayers to everyone. That's all we could do. The tragedy had happened and we couldn't bring anyone back; we could only honor them by remembering their lives.

All over town, 3407 was all that mattered. There were churches doing all kinds of memorials for the victims and their families. You'd walk into the coffee shop at the four corners and it was the topic of every conversation there, too. You'd look at somebody and smile at him or her, and before you knew it, you'd be giving each other a warm embrace. We didn't even have to know each other. We were just thankful and grateful for one another. We had to come together. We had to be strong. We had to endure a horrible thing that fortunately doesn't happen to most towns. A plane doesn't just crash into buildings and cause nameless, faceless casualties. A plane crashes through a community and takes away your loved ones, your friends and neighbors, your priest or rabbi, your coworkers, forever.

At home, I kept a close watch on Dave. Every night when he came home—when he could come home—we sat down and talked. That's still something we do every day, whether it's in the morning or at night. That's one of the strengths in our relationship: we talk. We sit down and hash out what's going on. When he comes home, I ask, "How are you feeling? What happened today?"

Throughout the incident, he kept telling me, "I'm doing okay." But I wasn't sure I believed him. I was looking intuitively for PTSD, searching for things that I think he was swallowing but didn't know he was swallowing. I don't know a lot about mental health, but I know when someone is hurting, so I wanted to establish routine emotional "checkpoints" as he worked the incident. Dave has been a firefighter since he was sixteen years old, so he has seen some pretty horrible accidents, things that most people would never see nor want to.

With this accident especially, I felt that I needed to check in with him to see if he was okay. Every time he said he was fine, I said, "Are you sure? Do you feel you need to talk to a mental-health specialist? It's the inward stuff, Dave, now. You've pushed back all of us who are feeling something because you don't want to feel it. You don't want to go there yet."

"I can't, Traci," he told me one night early on in the incident. "I've got a job to do. When I'm done with that job, we'll address it." I left him alone after that, but every day we would talk and I would give him a report, of sorts, on the hometown feeling. I would tell him what I was hearing at the salon and reading on social media, how so many people were saying how fantastic a job he was doing and how proud of him they were.

He was so deliberate and compassionate all at the same time, and that really touched people in town. It was really all of those things that people were saying to me that helped me—and also helped Dave—get stronger and stronger. I think that's the effect of the community when people with kind hearts open them up for others to find shelter.

When you go through any type of a disaster, you have your heart ripped open, and you have feelings exposed that aren't the norm. But it's amazing what incredible things can come from tragedy. That's the main reason we're writing this book together, because there are just so many wonderful things that we've learned from each other as human beings, experiencing the same feelings together at the same time. And yet, through that darkness came the light of humanity. Each of us is part of a collective heart. We all have the ability to serve the greater whole without questioning and without wanting anything in return. We had faith and hope that this incident would leave us stronger, somehow. Our love became stronger for all who helped, who gave of themselves freely. We knew there must be lessons, something larger than us—we just couldn't see it then.

MEMORIAL SERVICES—DAVE'S PERSPECTIVE

Traci's right about the community's impact on repairing the town's emotional state during this time. In the early stages, there was an immediate outpouring of support that came in the form of food donations for the first responders and volunteer-provided services and equipment. Everyone was making themselves available, which was a project in itself to collect, sort, and retain for future use. The second wave of support we observed was one of coping and grieving. Initiatives like memory ribbons tied around trees and telephone poles and lapel pins helped the community mourn in solidarity. Underlying efforts to recognize the lives lost and the families that lost them were as visible as they were inspiring.

There was the sustained public support for the operation. If an operation causes difficulty or the town's residents are not in agreement with the way things are being done, then it can turn against you in a hurry. Frankly, we're very quick to be critical of an operation, whether it's an emergency or a public project. But in this case, the residents and the town itself were very supportive. There was little resistance, if any, to how things were being done and why.

Instead, the community focused its attention on the memorials, setting up sites all over town to leave notes, flowers, stuffed animals, and other symbols of encouragement and respect. I was becoming more and more aware of various religious congregations holding and hosting services for the families and the community, each in their own religions. In particular, the Eastern Hills Wesleyan Church (which, at between two and three thousand members, had one of the biggest congregations in town at the time) brought everyone together for the purposes of a memorial ceremony. That was a huge event. I had very little knowledge about how it developed, as it was not part of my role or scope, but I was asked to attend alongside a few other dignitaries, and so I did.

I wasn't sure of my role in the memorial services. I remember thinking, *Should I be there when I need to be at my post and moving forward with the operation? Am I a **visual** leader as much as a **functional** leader at this point?* I struggled with that a bit, but ultimately Traci helped me make the right choice, and we did attend. I was so glad I did, as the message sent by not being there would have been detrimental to my compassionate-leadership attitude. People were expecting me to be running the operation, but they also wanted me to take the time to be present for events like that and show public support for our community and the victims' families. However, I needed to define my boundaries to keep from overstepping my role, so while I did go to the larger memorials, I did not go to many of the private ones.

For weeks after the incident, Traci and I went to as many public memorials and funeral services as we could. Even now, as I reflect on those services and the families involved, it's very emotional for me. In those moments, I was no longer a town official, not an emergency manager or a fire chief operating a tactical mission, either. All those roles fell away the moment I saw my friends, neighbors, colleagues, and wife in so much pain, and I was just like them: a person wracked with shock, questions, and sadness over the loss of so many human lives in a single instant. Traci had a client on that flight that had come in to get his hair done just two weeks before the plane crashed. She was stricken with grief personally. Even after all these years, the faces of the victims' families, the devastation and heartbreak written across them, remain vividly in my memory, perhaps implanted forever.

Memorials were also popping up throughout town, in the way of drop-offs for flowers and mementos. That was very touching to see, too, as it displayed the great need people felt to contribute something as we all mourned together.

The memorials became fairly routine experiences with the families and the communal sadness of the event, and they kept my role in perspective as I went back to the EOC. I knew, very clearly, why what we were doing mattered so much. It reinforced the need to be successful because we were consistently reminded of what the stakes were. When I stepped back into the EOC, I felt that I needed to address what I knew we were all feeling. So during one of our morning briefings, I started with a short comment. "We are so focused on the site and the deceased," I said, "but we also need to make sure we stay just as focused on the living."

CHAPTER 5

CLARENCE ON CALL: UNITED BY DISASTER

Community support is a big piece of the compassionate-leadership approach. Because Clarence Center is a small, suburban community, we tend to pull together with or without a mass tragedy looming overhead, but even large cities pull together when you give them a common need. In this situation, though, I think it's safe for me to say that everyone was looking in the mirror, so to speak. Residents recognized that this was a terrible situation happening in their own backyard, and they wanted to help heal the pain.

That effort was on display very early in the incident. Within the first few hours of impact, the neighborhood had been properly evacuated, with displaced residents mostly finding shelter with friends and family. Normally I would have had to provide a place for these people to go, but the level of community support was unbelievable. I didn't have to use my regular shelter options because of the help we were getting from our residents. Every time you get a freebie like that, it's a big shot in the arm and allows you to work on something more pressing.

Within the first twenty-four hours following the crash, it seemed like the whole town was checking in and asking, "How can I help? What do you need?" Offers for volunteers, monetary donations, food—you name it—poured in so heavily that we had to put someone in charge of collecting all the information so that we could come back to it later and not lose it. That was something that Traci volunteered to do without even being asked. I didn't know she was doing it until much later, but she took on that role and contributed greatly to the relief effort. That's exactly the kind of thing so many people did. They saw what needed to be done, and they took on the role to do it.

The blue-collar segment of the operation was particularly helpful, from the owner of a local construction company offering all his equipment, to a lumber mill offering materials, to the restaurants offering catering. All of that input gave us a much greater advantage as we worked to bring closure to the incident, at least from a tactical perspective. Plus, it was an opportunity for these guys to really get involved and say, "Here's what my skills and my knowledge can contribute." It was a time for so many people, many of whom don't usually get the chance, to really shine and show the community what they were capable of in a time of crisis. I was very proud of my community.

This incident took the average volunteerism impact and multiplied it by ten. When someone volunteers to do a task or provide something—whether it's a service or some other resource—that's part of his or her coping mechanism in a time of tragedy. Luckily for us, this level of volunteerism added a value to the response and recovery process that we never could have expected and certainly couldn't have demanded. Volunteers are critical in a smaller community like Clarence. They need to get involved, and in this case, they were yearning for a way to show that. You just have to give them a way to do it, which can become a whole job in itself.

VOLUNTEER MANAGEMENT

One trouble spot I remember happened fairly early on in the recovery. Within the first three or four days of the incident, we were having trouble with credentialing. Anyone going down to the scene had to have an actual *business* need. It took us a while, but we established a credentialing process. Credentialing involved a person going to the EOC at the town hall. Once they were acknowledged as a person or a function that was needed at the scene, we processed a credential so that he or she could get through security.

One man walked in and said, "I don't know if you need any help, but I have a background in identifications." IDs were a great need for us then, so I said, "Perfect."

I called over the head of resource operations and told him, "We're going to start a credentialing station this morning so we can get this whole credentialing thing under control. Maybe this guy would be willing to man that desk." So with the assistance of the state police, we set up a credentialing station for him to operate.

I never got his first name, nor do I know to this day exactly who he was, but he sat at that desk for three long days and did a bang-up job. He could have worked for the IRS. He could have worked for the customs department. I have no idea, but he did a great job and really helped us out when we needed that resource most.

Another example of community support through volunteerism was the fire department's informal Ladies' Auxiliary. The Clarence Center Firehouse was about 1,500 feet up the street from the crash, which made them easily accessible from the scene. At that firehouse, the Ladies' Auxiliary branch served three meals a day for the crash-site workers.

First responders could simply walk up the street to the fire hall and sit down and have their meals, every day for two weeks straight. During that time, particularly in the first half of the incident, there were 250, maybe even 300, people in their banquet room daily, having meals served by the Ladies' Auxiliary of the fire hall.

I had always known about the Ladies' Auxiliaries organization from other fire halls, however, Clarence Center has a very strong, active group of women consisting of wives and girlfriends of the fire-fighters. They produced four to five hundred meals a day, completely as volunteers. They were not a catering group, nor were they being paid. They set up their own shifts and had people coming and going so that there was never interruption, always ensuring that there was a warm place to sit and have a hot meal. That in itself was amazing to me.

I visited that kitchen early on and spoke to one of the leading women there to let her know I had a catering company on call that would come down and take over so they didn't have to keep working so hard. She told me, "Absolutely not." She would hear nothing of anyone taking over their role. They wanted to do this job, and they were going to do it as long as it needed to be done.

So I just looked at her and said, "Okay then," and I turned around and walked out. There was no need for me to be there anymore. From both a human-needs and mental-health perspective, that type of volunteer initiative was a big piece of keeping the community involved and feeling valuable during a tragic emergency. I can't say enough about the work that those ladies did.

Without question and without missing a beat, they did an outstanding job, and they did it for as long as was necessary. They were all a huge asset to the incident, and we greatly appreciated their tremendous efforts to help keep us going.

The town hall had many people coming to make food donations as well. Many of the law enforcement agencies were there, and thanks to the generosity of the community and local restaurants, food kept coming in at a high volume. Traci was there helping out, and she realized she needed some refrigeration, so she called Brian Perry, owner of Perry's Ice Cream, for some refrigerator trucks to store all of the food donations, and he very graciously provided them on a moment's notice.

Restaurants and grocery stores in towns nearby also sent food— so much of it, in fact, that volunteers traded off on a full-time job just to coordinate that resource. Other donations came in from equipment vendors and rental companies. We needed many different types of equipment tactically on-scene: heaters, lights, cranes, rigging, heavy machinery, front-end loaders, excavators, etc., and most of those things came in as donations at that time. Later on, we were to repay some of those bigger contractors for their expenses, but initially, they were all volunteer assets. The camaraderie was palpable. Truly amazing.

We needed that kind of help too, to be honest. Clarence isn't a big city with hundreds of employees you can just delegate or defer to a problem. These were regular people who were willing to take on a tough job, if you just told them what you needed and gave them what they required to do the job. Most of them I didn't know, and I didn't need to. People came along, identified themselves, and we put them to work. I couldn't have asked for a better community response than the one we received during that very difficult time for us all.

That's the way things should be every day when people work together in this way. Personal satisfaction from the response mission was at an all-time high in town, whether you were directly involved or on the periphery. That kind of emotional support is a huge part of what gets both first responders and residents through the trauma of a terrible situation.

MENTAL HEALTH AND THE FIRST RESPONDER

When the mental fatigue and stress of a traumatic incident are more serious than a home-cooked meal or basic acts of human kindness can resolve, then we have to seek the help of a professional. We understood that from the beginning of the Flight 3407 incident, and we wanted to make sure we had resources available to properly address the mental health of our first responders, volunteers, and the public in general.

Mental health has been something the first-responder community has been addressing for many years. This is not a new subject, as first responders experience stressful and emotional events nearly every day in their communities. In most crises, whether it's a family member or a public event, there's a lot at stake for one's quality of life, and lost lives are obviously an extremely emotional exposure.

First responders typically have services available to them, such as critical-stress debriefing programs by local county and state health officials. In the private sector, there are also mental-health professionals available to help a first responder cope with his or her exposure. Despite the availability, traditional firefighters and law-enforcement officers have not typically engaged in mental-health services, because it was uncool to do so. There is, after all, the whole "tough guy" mentality to contend with—but taking care of your mind after absorbing so much emotional strain on a daily basis is nothing to be ashamed of. Because it so regularly seems to be, however, first responders often go home and avoid talking about their lengthy exposure to stress and trauma until it ends up surfacing in their personal lives in the way of frustration, insensitivity, and even violence in some cases.

When I went home most days, I was not approachable or really paying attention to what Traci was saying. It's likely I was restraining my emotions. I had become so guarded that interacting with others as I normally would became unusually difficult, and I didn't appear to be emotionally present. These are all red flags for critical-stress issues.

We wanted to make our first responders and our public aware of those red flags, and we wanted them to know where to turn to for help, whether it was working through that particular incident or some other stressor. Not properly addressing the issue by talking it out with a professional only compounds the risks associated with emotional trauma and prolonged, intense mental stress.

Due to the scale and nature of flight 3407—the enormous loss of life, and the grueling operation itself—the incident was emotionally very difficult and certainly made for a case in which mental health was a priority during and after the mission.

Thankfully, many of the first responders attended the critical-stress debriefings, as well as counseling services that were being offered through their own fire departments, thanks to the Erie County Health Department, members of the area clergy, and others in the community who were able to provide that kind of expertise.

As for myself, the first session I attended was at the end of phase one, when the first departments were starting to scale down and hand the scene over to the next group. I started getting involved with the fire department because those are the people I know best. That first briefing was when I really began to think about all the people who had died. And it became overwhelming for me when I thought about all the lives that had been permanently changed by their deaths.

I started asking myself, as many of us did, *Could I have done anything more?* It was a pretty short conversation in that case, as there really was nothing else we could have done. We couldn't have gotten there any quicker, and even if we had, there still wouldn't have been any survivors for us to rescue. That made it a little easier, knowing that we had done everything we could within our power to save lives and minimize the pain and agony of the victims' loved ones.

I will admit that I found myself going to these mental-health sessions, initially, as a *leader*. It was one thing for me to strongly recommend or mandate that everyone go to at least one critical stress debriefing session—but if the guy in charge didn't go, then what does that mean? It's do as I do, not as I say. So, while at first I went to a few sessions just to be a good leader, I ended up receiving a lot of helpful personal answers for myself. Everyone had a different perspective; I don't think any two were the same, except that most everyone seemed to be most affected by the loss of life. For me, the greatest comfort of all was just to hear the different perspectives of my colleagues and friends.

Some people were really upset by the fact that families were displaced. "When they come home, they're going to be coming home to a crash scene." We talked about that a lot, that the neighborhood would never be the same. We could fix the grass, fix the street, and everything else, but the emotional scars would always be there. What we learned as a coping mechanism was to understand the limits of direct control. I can influence outcomes, and I will, but most incidents are out of my control. I can be okay with that as long as I can tell myself that I've done everything possible. If I can do that, then I've done my best.

We were also really careful not to alienate any worker or member of the public who sought counseling or, in the case of first responders, attended critical-stress debriefings. No one was singled out. We all went through it together and pulled together to work through it as a family.

When it came to the town employees and the first responders, there was some mandate to the process. Otherwise, we worried that it would be too casual and we wouldn't have a good turnout. The supervisor made it a mandate that everyone had to go. Did we get 100 percent attendance? Probably not, but the lion's share of the town's employees and the first-response personnel all attended the sessions and understood that the purpose was to help them cope. There were also people who were there because they had concerns but didn't feel a need to talk. They were simply there to help others who wanted to talk. You can put everyone in at least one of those categories to get them there, which is a great strategy for getting good attendance: give everyone a place to belong in the process.

We also had county health workers available, and we opened one of our primary shelters in town to the public, for purposes of emotional counseling and coaching. I had been getting a lot of feedback from residents around town, in many cases from parents asking me what they should tell their children, or hearing from others that the young people in town were having a difficult time processing the tragedy. There was a lot going on casually around town as well. People were really looking for this conversation with a group, and they seemed to be leaning on each other at the local coffeehouses and restaurants rather than mental-health professionals. Obviously that can create even more confusion and grief, so we wanted to make sure the public was getting answers from the right people in a professional setting. All of those factors generated my need to have at least one location where a person could go and talk to someone if he or she wanted to. I don't honestly know how many people ever showed up at the shelter, but we made sure that it was in place should the public need it or want it.

CHAPTER 6

FEEDING THE
MEDIA FRENZY

Media relations were a big part of my role as emergency coordinator. While the rest of the process was still coming together, I needed to continue conveying what was going on, what we knew, and what we didn't know, to the public.

The role the PIO has in providing calm for the public, as well as information that doesn't require a retraction later on, is extremely important to the overall success of the mission. Once you're news, you and your operation will either be praised or condemned, labeled a proficient hero or an incompetent villain, and reversing either depiction will likely never happen. In the media game, you are defined almost entirely by your first impression and the presumptions that spiral from it. If you don't make the media your friendly ally in the very beginning, then you've made a powerful opponent, and only one of you holds the microphone. We knew that, and because of it, we spent a lot of time making sure we had regularly scheduled press releases.

Another important piece for us was to establish our media area away from the EOC, so we were not drawing confusion and distraction to the work going on there.

The press conferences were, by design, intended to be short and to-the-point. We didn't spend a lot of time on the Q&A segments. We always left time for questions, but we kept our answers brief and specific. The idea was to convey current information coming from the appropriate agency representatives on the subject in question.

Establishing interview protocol was also very important to me. I knew this was going to be a long-term relationship with the media, so I made sure that they understood it wasn't going to be a circus, that there was going to be a specific process with ground rules as I went around the press team answering questions and taking feedback.

As we were getting into days three and four, I had time to look at some of the finer details of our media relations. The use of *media pools* was something new that I tried as a result. We began taking small groups of media down to the scene to take pictures and collect information, which they would then bring back and distribute among their colleagues. To avoid disrupting the operation, this was only a handful of people whom I would personally escort around the scene. And the next day, I would take a different group down. So each day a different set of people shared their experiences with their counterparts. That seemed to satiate the media pretty well and quickly became a best practice for us.

Sensitivity to the families of the victims and the residents in the town remained my priority in my relations with the media. We were becoming a national focus in a very short amount of time, so if we didn't give them accurate, routine information, they were going to find it themselves through whatever means possible. Even with our two-a-day press conferences, I had members of the media literally cutting their way through heavy, dense brush to come around behind the incident in search of a story. My first concern was that someone was going to get hurt. My second was that they were going to start interviewing people who would give them inaccurate information and cause some unintended harm to the families. That didn't happen often, and it really subsided after the first few days, but it was something we certainly had to react to quickly.

Once we found a rhythm with the media and established our authority over the incident as a story, they really became our greatest tool to reach the public. You don't hear very many emergency-services managers say that, but that may be because we often approach the media all wrong.

For most of my career, even, the media was way down on my list of things to deal with or be concerned about. My objectives were solely preserving life and protecting property. Telling everyone about what was going on was not on my list of concerns. But as I matured as an emergency manager, the media became far more important to public awareness and factual information. People have an insatiable appetite to be informed about what's going on in their community, however you wish to define that, and they most certainly will be informed by some form of media. The problem is misinformation, whether intentional or unintentional. We don't want people to be so frustrated by a lack of information, particularly when it's affecting their quality of life, that they begin accepting bad information. So keeping the public informed becomes a value-added condition to the overall incident.

With that in mind, I sought to use the media as a positive asset, not to only keep the public informed but also to keep the media in check. I'm not coming down on the media, either. Reporters have a job to do, and that's to report the news. What I do object to, though, is the media finding creative ways of crossing security lines, taking information from unauthorized sources, reporting speculation as news—and other practices that are unacceptable and unprofessional. Those types of reporting techniques actually cause more confusion and discontent in the public because now they're getting mixed information and even plain false information.

That's the reason why, for years, those of us in emergency management tended to avoid the media—but I now urge emergency managers and first responders to embrace the media. They're going to be there anyway, so use them to your advantage. Make them an asset and a resource, rather than a problem to be constantly managed. When you use the media as your megaphone, you can ensure that the information you want to get out to the public gets out when and how you want. For this incident in particular, we were able to generate a relationship that we could count on throughout the operation, and I was even able to call in a few favors later on to get word out to the public about one event or another. The media is going to find a story regardless, whether you give it to them or not. We wanted to make sure they had a story to tell, and we wanted to make sure it was coming from our mouths—the designated people in charge of the operation—and not someone else's.

Plus, the faster that the media gets what it needs and leaves, pretty much indefinitely, the faster we can begin putting that energy into other things more pertinent to the long-term goals of the incident.

SOCIAL MEDIA

Social media had become a major source of information and dissemination by that time (2009) as well, although there was relatively little of it in comparison with what's out there today. I knew I couldn't afford to have people—even other first responders—trying to answer a question because someone with a camera and a microphone was asking. Human nature would suggest that when you have that uncontrollable urge to answer a question, you answer it with whatever you know, and that's when we start to get misinformation, that inaccurate or just plain incorrect feedback going out to the masses. Accurate information, with no retractions, that's the goal! So we want it to be a single source, and we want it to be thoughtful to whatever the situation is. And in this case, of course, it was the significant life loss.

Social media posed a new kind of challenge for us, with its on-the-spot questions and answers being broadcast live, with very little editing, to be shared over and over again, whether by text or e-mail, tweets, blogs, or personal-sharing platforms such as Facebook. As that information is shared, it gains momentum and builds like a snowball.

To combat what could have become a confusing and disruptive phenomenon, it's important today to assign a social media liaison within the operation to satisfy that stream of information. Again, this person should be sharing only the proper information. Obviously, emergency managers can't control all communications between those involved in a given operation and the general public, but we should stay vigilant and work to prevent different information circulating in different media streams.

During our incident, I made a decision a couple of days in to keep an eye on social media and restrict the use of smart phones on-site. We'd already had a problem with first responders taking pictures with their phones and releasing them on their Facebook accounts, as well as texting from the scene. That could not happen! This was a secure location and needed to remain so. And if nothing else, out of respect for the families of the deceased, we certainly couldn't have fireground scene pictures going viral.

After I made the decision that we weren't going to allow cell phones in the hot zone, I received some pushback from law enforcement concerning the logistics of policing cell phones on-scene. "Well, how do you expect us to enforce this?" a state police captain asked. "We're not going to go searching every first responder for a phone."

"No," I said, "but when you see phones out, I want them put away or removed from the scene. If they're not going to put the phones away, then *they've* got to go."

This particular captain didn't like that, as he thought I was making life unnecessarily difficult during an already difficult situation. His boss agreed with me, however, and that was that. Those became his orders to follow, and we never heard another word about it. The captain and I even had a big laugh over it later. He hadn't known who I was when he first refused to follow my plan, but after he went home that night he saw a news conference in which I was briefing the press. The next day, he started laughing when he saw me and said, "Great. I just got into an argument with the guy running the whole thing." We are good friends to this day.

We didn't have a lot of rumors coming from the accident scene. This was a large-scale disaster with so much devastation already that no one was looking to cause more problems; that would have been a poor career choice for any professional. Fortunately, the overwhelming majority of the first-responder community—EMS, fire, law enforcement—respects the chain of command and the role of the public information officer very definitively.

LET ME DO THE TALKING

The other thing I speak a lot about now is the role of the public information officer. Prior to 3407, I would have said the PIO is someone we need to designate. But now I believe that this person needs to be both comfortable with the media and with being the face of the incident. For a one- or two-hour event, the PIO is the one who's reporting on the situation and answering questions for the media. But if it's an ongoing incident over an extended period of time, then you are now the face of that entire incident.

What I didn't recognize, or hadn't recognized up to that point in my career, was that when you are repeatedly the face of something, whether good, bad, or otherwise, you will always be known for it. There's a notoriety that goes along with the event. It could be good. It could be bad. If the event is going poorly and has lost credibility with the public, then you can become the face of negative notoriety very quickly. If it's going well and the incident has credibility, then there's a pride that comes along with it and a certain amount of positive notoriety, which is fortunately what happened to me.

But be careful who you put in that role. We don't know how it's going to go until it's over. Will this person be able to handle a negative outcome, God forbid it should occur? Most people can handle the positive by working through it, but the negative can be very detrimental on a personal level.

CHAPTER 7

THE LITTLE TOWN
THAT COULD

DAY FOUR: SUNDAY, FEBRUARY 15, 2009

By the fourth day, I still didn't have line of sight as to how long the tasks associated with the aftermath of the incident might take. I was getting feedback from NTSB and several state assets that we were looking at a four- to six-week operation and that I would have to pace myself. When I was told that, my response was immediate: "There's no way in hell we're going to be working on this for six weeks. We're going to do everything possible we can every day until this is done." When dealing with something as high profile as this event, it's only a matter of time before mistakes are made and shouted across the globe. I knew we were playing against some very strong odds that something would go horribly wrong. I wanted to minimize those chances as much as possible, and the only way to do that was to get out of the hot seat as quickly as possible.

I had overseen my share of commercial construction projects, so I had a gauge as to a reasonable time frame. I remained confident that I could coordinate a faster cleanup than what was being estimated. I believed that, once we passed the sensitivity of recovery and entered the remediation phase of the operation, we could tackle the incident like a construction project. I knew the right people to put in the right places, and I knew our local agencies were particularly driven to get our neighbors back into their homes sooner rather than later.

We would continue having our planning sessions and briefs among agencies, particularly during the remediation phase. I made it very clear that we were going to be working around the clock, 24/7, until everyone was home and out of harm's way. I did back off within a couple of days because the weather was pretty lousy, but I agreed to work eighteen-hour days to make up for the difference. The point I wanted to make was that we weren't going to be letting up until the job was done. I had nothing else I needed to do, so there was no other focus for me than to keep things moving forward.

I was very fortunate to have Traci's support and understanding during this time, as well as that of General Mills. I had had encouraging phone calls very early on with the General Mills headquarters in Minneapolis. Even senior vice presidents and directors called me, along with the plant manager in Buffalo, to say, "Look, we see what's going on. We see you on CNN. You're doing a great job. Is there anything General Mills can do for you?" I remember telling one VP, "First of all, thank you, but we've got a good plan here. If you just assure me my job is there when this is over, we'll be good." We both laughed, and they couldn't have been more supportive about the tragedy that was left for us to bring to a tactical close.

Between my personal life and my livelihood, I had complete freedom to give my undivided attention to the operation at hand.

We spent eleven days working nonstop on this to get the residents back into their homes—and two weeks after that, I still had significant follow-ups to oversee. Throughout it all, I had full support from Traci, the town of Clarence, General Mills, and hundreds of volunteers, contractors, and emergency-services personnel. It goes without saying, but not having that support would have made it far more difficult to achieve success.

KEEPING IN TOUCH

As we began going into overdrive on fumes, I wanted to stay connected with the residents in Clarence. There were a lot of realizations coming into play around town after four days of absorbing so much trauma. Part of my compassionate-leadership strategy was dedicated to public perception, morale, and sensitivity to the residents of Clarence, not just on Long Street, but in general. Everyone was feeling a loss—a frustrated loss because there was little they could do about it. This terrible thing happened, in our town no less, and people take that very personally. When something like this happens in a town, the residents feel like it happened to them.

Traci played a big role in keeping me reminded of our sensitivity to the public. One of the things she urged me to do was to hold a town hall meeting. As soon as Traci pitched the idea to me, I knew we had to do it. "Yeah, I can do that. That's something we should do."

When I proposed it to the town supervisor, however, he didn't think it was such a great idea. To him, this felt like it could have the potential for the public to blow up and get ugly about whatever they were not happy about. That was certainly a risk. But I looked at it as an opportunity to do a health check on our progress with the public. A town hall meeting would give me a chance to ask the residents about our weak spots directly: "How are we doing? What have you heard, and what do you need to know? Are we missing critical services, or are we missing a critical subject and not addressing something?"

Because school was not in session, I was able to take the Clarence High School auditorium and turn it into a town hall forum. At that time, there were fourteen key agencies working on the incident, and I invited a representative from each one to join our discussion. We put a bunch of tables and chairs up on the stage, and when it was all said and done, each agency had a representative sitting on the stage.

We sent out invitations explicitly to the town of Clarence residents and made sure that no media was permitted in the auditorium. Close to four hundred people came with questions, concerns, or just their own curiosity to hear what we had to say. We set up a podium and microphone in the middle of the auditorium and allowed people to come forward with their comments. We had a scribe write down each person's name and contact number, and then they were each given three minutes to ask a question or make a statement.

I served as the forum's mediator and made sure there were no politicians on the stage, only operational leadership. I did that because I wanted to ensure that no political grandstanding or finger-pointing took place. Instead, I wanted this to be an opportunity for the town to be together as people to discuss their fears, worries, support, criticisms, or whatever else was on their minds. "I want you to know that I live in this town, too, so our success is as personal for me as it is for you," I said shortly after taking the stage. I wanted them to know that I was one of them, and I wanted their help in learning how this incident was going and how it could be better.

As I recall, we went for about an hour and a half to two hours, answering several questions and responding to the concerns of a dozen or so residents. "What will happen with pollution, and who will monitor that potential?" someone asked. "When can we return to our homes?" asked another. "Who's responsible for cleaning up the neighborhood? Who's going to pay for things?" They were all good questions, and we were able to answer just about every one of them right then and there. Because I tend to be very tactical in my thought process, I always need to have a reason for what I'm doing, always asking myself, *What am I doing here? What is my purpose? What does success look like with regard to the subject at hand?* That thought process isn't the best for every situation, but it played well with the nature of the Q&A. All the audience really wanted was completion, so we wanted the same thing. But it was the *how* that I needed to make sure I understood from their perspective.

By the end, all four hundred people seemed satisfied with the new information, and despite the apprehension that the event would turn into a public flogging, it was a tremendous success for us. We had an opportunity to shed light on any issues that the public was not aware of, but more importantly, we were able to calm fears created by some of the scuttlebutt that was either not true or not completely accurate.

New York State Governor Patterson made a visit a couple of days later. We had a press conference at the Erie County Training Academy which is, again, just outside of town limits. I made my visit, shook his hand, and we talked for a couple of minutes. I wanted to keep my distance from political affiliations, so I let the county and the state people do their own thing with the governor. Any constituency expects to see its emergency leadership in a time of mass tragedy, but they don't really want to hear from it. They want you to know that you're being recognized as a need, but they really don't want you to get involved as a political leader. I understood that, even welcomed that sentiment, and excused myself shortly after meeting the governor and went back to the EOC to resume operational duties.

As far as negative public interactions during the incident went, I was fortunate to have been spared almost entirely from public backlash. Unless someone was actually sheltering me from bad press, I only had one nasty e-mail directed at me after I pleaded with the public not to visit the crash scene to see what happened. I made the comment during an early press release, stating that gawkers would only slow down our process and delay getting the disaster under control.

Someone took real exception to me calling the public "gawkers," writing, "We're taxpayers, and you have no business referring to the public as gawkers." I could live with that, and so could the town supervisor. He brought the printed e-mail to me with a smile on his face, and we both had to chuckle to keep from fuming. The priorities some people have during a time in which so much more is at stake for others can never be predicted.

Everywhere else I went, I got nothing but reasonable conversation and positive support. Almost a year after the incident, local residents still showed their gratitude by buying me a cup of coffee, shaking my hand, or, on one occasion, even buying dinner for several friends and me. Even today, I still have people come up to me and express their gratitude for the work we did. There aren't enough words for how that makes you feel. To have the public's support and recognition is beyond humbling.

CHAPTER 8

REMEDIATION BEGINS

DAY FIVE: MONDAY, FEBRUARY 16, 2009

As the investigation heated up, more and more hands were needed to assist the ME's office as it combed the scene to recover victims and relevant clues. Additional agencies were also arriving around the time we expanded the operation to include contractor support, ranging from heavy equipment, to laborers, to transportation. The ME's office also had to train more hands for the recovery operations. All these new needs meant that we needed to navigate a line change, of sorts, as new roles were created and new agencies with new faces and personalities were introduced.

The ME's office decided to recruit assistants from Mercyhurst College in Pennsylvania, which is about a hundred miles southwest of Clarence. These were third-year forensics students, but with the MEs struggling to acquire qualified manpower, they needed to train as many technical hands as possible, and they needed to do it in a matter of hours. With options running low, the students offered the best solution for overcoming that shortage.

The law-enforcement agencies were starting to shift gears as well, with officers moving in and out on a rotation-based schedule, particularly the state police. They had well over two hundred troopers moving through the operation, and now they were drawing from all over the state for job rotations here in Clarence. The local police agencies, particularly the Erie County Sheriff's Department, were still tasked with day-to-day operations, but they funneled extra help over to us in a rotational structure. This stage provided our first wide look at the incident's long-term effects on the first responders. Human limits were beginning to be reached, and if we didn't find ways to rotate the roster with fresh responders or provide breaks to the current rotational system, then the whole operation would be at risk.

As the operation approached the one-week mark, the investigation began to wind down and the remediation phase, the final phase of emergency response, loomed. Most of the brass was starting to disappear as the novelty of the incident waned, and our adrenaline was now long gone, replaced with exhaustion and a renewed commitment to finish the job. People were starting to look for their exit strategy, so the leadership had to keep the incident moving along at a good clip to avoid having idle hands, which turn into idle conversations, which can ultimately turn into undermining key objectives.

DAY SIX: TUESDAY, FEBRUARY 17, 2009

Because of that exhaustion, the remediation phase couldn't have come at a better time for us. Remediation—for those wondering—is the last phase of any crisis incident, and it typically involves a new cast of professionals. Technically speaking, it's the basic clean-up portion of an incident, and so it was for us as well. By this point, the other agencies had gotten their information and exited the scene, so the focus was purely on putting the community back together again. For me, the remediation phase marked the point at which I was able to take a bit of a breath and recognize that we were on the downside of this monster. I had been keeping two or three steps ahead of the actual field progress to stay timely, yet accurate, in my planning strategy, so the last day or so of the recovery phase was my green light to start putting the remediation team together. I had all the information I was going to need to address the next steps. I also knew my construction background and experience would come in handy during the remediation phase, so I approached it just as I would have a construction job: I devised and adhered to a critical-task schedule and choreographed a variety of contractors and key players as we moved from one task to the next.

I first established a remediation team that comprised regulatory agencies, specifically the Department of Environment and Conservation (DEC). The DEC is an agency that provides oversight on contamination, hazardous materials, residuals, and anything relative to the environment. In addition to the DEC, the Town of Clarence department heads from code enforcement, the highway department, and the parks department were also on the team. Rounding out the remediation roster were outside agencies and contractors for environmental testing and cleanup for whatever residuals we found.

One of my strategies was to put the DEC in charge of the remediation phase under my guidance and support. Some have been curious about that decision, but its explanation is really quite simple. I did it because the DEC was the regulatory agency that would be confirming and qualifying the work that was to be done. From my perspective, who better to put in charge of the task than the people who will judge the accuracy and success of the task? That was a successful strategy in that the DEC head representatives, along with the town building department, had a great oversight perspective on what needed to be done to make these properties safe and legal. They brought along their understanding of remediation tasks, as well as the resources and contractors required to bring success to each one. They also had their own list of approved contractors and were able to bring those contract relationships into our project, which saved me from having to find contractors who were qualified to do this work.

Additionally, at this phase in the incident, resources were starting to dry up. All the volunteers (such as the contractors and the businesses) were starting to get tired and withdraw from the operation. So, for this last phase, most of the workers were fresh faces with fresh energy because their expertise hadn't been a part of the process until now. Frankly, everyone who had been there since the beginning was already pretty whipped. The New York State Department of Environmental Conservation (DEC) is not known for any favoritism. They choose contractors based on a round-robin system to keep it impartial, and because of this fact, I felt comfortable handing the hiring process over to them.

DAY SEVEN: WEDNESDAY, FEBRUARY 18, 2009

With the team assembled, we began the remediation by taking physical samples around the site for a number of things: toxins, fuel and fuel-residual contamination, organic hazards, etc. Once we had those results, we shifted our focus to two buildings on the neighboring sides of the crash. One had been irreparably damaged and would need to be demolished, after all salvageable personal items had been packaged and put into storage. Before the demolition could proceed, we had to test the home for lead and asbestos to ensure that building debris could go to a landfill, and we also had to test the soil around the condemned structure for ground pollution.

Collecting and testing the samples took a day and a half, which was extremely efficient given the amount of samples that needed to be extracted and processed. The test results supported the fact that there were no pollution concerns. We had predicted that most of the aircraft fuel had burned up in the crash, and that proved to be substantially correct. The demolished house had some toxic contents in it, but they were known, and we were able to collect and abate those materials in a timely fashion. The testing data confirmed that we hadn't missed anything or left anything behind from the investigation and recovery phase.

Meanwhile, media communication remained an everyday responsibility. Some national media and most of the global media had pretty much disappeared by the end of the recovery and the investigation, but local, regional, and a handful of national media crews were still in town and needed to stay informed on our progress. The remediation phase was of particular interest in the Northeast and certainly locally, as people wanted to know when their community would be returned to everyday life. More importantly, this phase especially mattered to the evacuees, all of whom were waiting anxiously to find out when, or if, they could move back into their homes.

Sixteen homes in all had been affected by the incident, but seven of those had been returned to the owners by this point. That left nine family homes that remained closed and whose occupants remained displaced. That aspect of the remediation progress made this final phase extremely important to me and the rest of the EOC. It had been just over a week at this point. If you're living with friends and family, you're asking yourself, *How much longer can I live like this?* You're trying to have something close to a normal life day to day, but it's becoming increasingly difficult to do so, especially for those who lost all or most of their possessions. That may not have been a matter of national interest—but it was just as important, if not more so, because these were the people I lived with. They weren't members of the national and international audience who wanted to come along through their television for the experience; these were the people I saw every day who wanted to go home, or at least to what was left of it. That's a different kind of pressure—a concern about stopping too soon or quitting short of the goal and returning a less-than-acceptable condition to the residents.

At the same time, I needed to make the neighborhood safe again. There were no residuals on surfaces, so we power washed the houses from the peak all the way to the ground. Then we removed surface contamination by taking up the grass and a couple inches of topsoil from the front yards of all the houses in the remediated area. In round terms, we were sanitizing, in various ways, approximately twelve acres of residential property.

I have to say, as well, that our crews showed exceptional sensitivity and dedication to the scene during the clean-up portion of this phase. The basement of the Wielinski house, for instance, was literally "broom cleaned," with just a few big hunks of concrete left. It had originally been a two-and-a-half-story home, but now it was transformed to a forty-foot-high pile of rubble that was sorted hand over hand, all the way down to the bottom of the foundation. That's what a crew of 350 or so people working sixteen-hour days for four days straight can accomplish. It's true to me, especially now, that much more can be accomplished with the human spirit than many people believe.

In addition to the personal attention to the site itself, we operated sieves and strainers to sift through debris and ground. Both the ME's office and the NTSB employees were filling five-gallon pails and bringing them over to garbage cans with quarter-inch screening boxes attached to them. Just like an archaeological dig, crews would then sift back and forth to reveal all objects larger than a grain of sand. We were able to return personal effects like wedding rings, earrings, and bracelets by doing so, which I think speaks to the compassion our on-site recovery crews brought to the overall operation. The surviving families were completely overwhelmed that we could return that amount of detail to them. I think I speak for everyone involved when I say that *that* experience, in particular, was very emotional for us.

Along with being sensitive to the victims' families and the displaced residents during remediation, a compassionate-leadership strategy also meant being sensitive to the local business community. We have a small-town environment here in Clarence, as I've said before, and the area surrounding the crash site also has a lot of small businesses embedded in it. Those businesses were separated from the public throughout the incident response. Obviously, if you're running a small business that's lost eleven days of business, that's a pretty serious shortfall.

To help alleviate some of those businesses' losses, I spent a lot of time with law enforcement to provide periodic and limited public access to the affected shops while not slowing down the remediation process. We also worked to pick up the garbage, deliver mail, and offer parking for the public to come and shop. Granted, there weren't a lot of people thinking about shopping right then, but all the local businesses really appreciated the effort later on, and it helped push our sense of overall success in the mission.

Once the sweat-equity had been paid, we had to finalize the paperwork before the incident could officially end. Even though the DEC was the lead agency, they were holding all of the other agencies and the contractors accountable for a regulatory-approved conclusion. The DEC and the town's code-enforcement inspectors would conduct a final check to ensure we had done everything that needed to be done safely, soundly, and legally. Only then could we turn the properties back over to their owners.

Thankfully, we passed our inspections without any complications, and on February 23—eleven days after I got that first call at home—Flight 3407's last check was complete. From a technical perspective, she could finally be laid to rest. But for those who helped to bury her, she did not go quietly.

DAY TWELVE: FEBRUARY 24, 2009

The conclusion didn't happen all at once. There was no ceremonial ribbon cutting or any fanfare event to mark the end of the nightmare and usher displaced residents home. It wasn't that crisp, because the nightmare was, of course, still lingering. The physical end of the incident, though, did come on day twelve—because that was the first day we could open the streets and return residents to their property.

For me, however, the delineation point between working the emergency and getting the town back to normal was when we could reopen traffic to the subdivision where the crash had occurred. By that definition, the real closure for the overall operation happened weeks later. Why? Because even after we finished with the incident and all the crews and equipment had picked up and gone, we still had to leave that subdivision closed to general traffic for a little more than a week to protect the neighborhood from uninvited guests hoping to visit the scene.

There was ongoing media and public interest for a few weeks after the remediation, which contributed to our delay as well. The entire world had been hearing about this crash, and now that everyone was gone, the next concern was the crushing interest by the public to come and see the site where it all happened. After all the global news interest, certainly the area residents wanted to see exactly what this event was for themselves. That was a big stressor for the local residential public.

How are we ever going to have quiet here anymore? I wondered, *particularly for the next few weeks or a month?* The public now knew that the streets were open for business, and people did come. So we had to have a law-enforcement presence there for weeks to keep people moving along and prevent them from parking on the residents' lawns to see what had happened.

I made a commitment to myself, and the supervisor made a commitment to the residents in that area, that we were not going to let that happen. Between the state police and the sheriff's department, we agreed we would have a presence there for at least a week after the incident was terminated to try to maintain some sanity for the residents. That subtle presence actually remained for a couple of weeks after that to maintain order in the area, and we were able to keep outside intrusion down to a very limited problem.

The town supervisor, the code-enforcement officer, and I had the luxury to escort, almost by appointment, each resident back to his or her home. I remember one senior citizen, who I believe lived by herself, meeting us at the town hall before returning to her home. Together, the four of us went to her house, tried the water, checked the phone, and made sure everything was working properly. She had put her trust in us for the last two weeks to take care of everything she had, and after all this work and effort, we were able to personally return her home to her. That was very emotional for me, and despite my discomfort with doing so, I gave her a big hug as we were leaving. She was appreciative of our attention to detail and for not leaving her with a mess to have to deal with, particularly on a limited income and with limited physical ability. The last thing she needed was a whole list of problems to follow up on over the next weeks and months, and she couldn't have been more grateful that she didn't have to worry anymore.

On the other hand, we couldn't fix everything. There was a family that lived right across the street from the crash site. They had small children and had some reservations about whether they wanted to be in the house or move away. It was their sense of security they were struggling to rebuild, and it was upsetting to see that there was still that much fear remaining in a family that had once felt so safe and happy.

MISSION COMPLETE: SHUTTING DOWN AND CLOSING UP

When we began the remediation phase, I was only dealing with a couple of environmental contractors and general contractors operating heavy equipment to repair the site. But during that time, the interaction among firefighters and law-enforcement officers off-scene was one of real camaraderie and pride, as well. Everyone had developed a bond, and that brotherhood attitude we often talk about so much was never stronger. That lasted for about two years, two years of recognizing faces that were there on that day and throughout that first week.

Personally, I crossed paths with all kinds of people all over western New York who either knew me or whom I knew. One of us would say, "Hey, I worked with you at that 3407 scene," and then there would be a handshake or a hug. Again, I'm not a big hugger, but that brotherhood, that common experience few can relate to, has remained very powerful to me.

The full-time professionals who worked this incident from the beginning have come and gone. We now have new personnel coming in to replace the original responders of 3407, so interactions are reverting to the solely professional instead of the brotherly common bond that results from a large-scale incident. Nonetheless, we still run into one another on occasion and find that the camaraderie has sustained itself all these years later.

On a personal level, however, processing 3407 was more difficult. For months after the incident, I lived in a shell. I felt alone, for the most part, because I didn't recognize anyone who I could talk to closely. Certainly, there was the command staff I had been tied to for those two weeks—close friends who became even dearer friends later on; but I still withdrew. To be that pumped up and in a somewhat defensive mode for weeks took a toll on me, and I grappled with letting go after it was all over.

Traci was tirelessly encouraging during this time, and truthfully, I don't know how I could have reconnected with the life we had shared prior to 3407 without her support and understanding. Nevertheless, I was stuck in a bit of a vacuum for a while. It was hard to turn that professional mind-set on and off just because I walked in the door at the end of the day. I think it was probably three or four months before I started becoming a "regular"-conversation kind of guy again.

In fact, I don't even remember a good portion of that month or so after the crash. I felt numb to everything, completely relieved of any feelings: good, bad, or otherwise. But while my personal life was pretty much at a standstill, Traci—who was also feeling the stresses from the experience—found some satisfaction and security with a group she was working with at the time.

I, on the other hand, was really just existing day to day. I had taken a week off from work before I went back to General Mills to try to gather my thoughts, but it wasn't going as well as I'd hoped. For the most part, General Mills had been great, saying to me in so many words, "Once this is all over, if you need some time, whatever you need to do, don't worry about it. Take the time." I used some of the week trying to come to grips with what we had just experienced. Unfortunately, even with the time off, everything was still a total blur as I tried to return to my previous life. I remember my first day back to work: I walked up to my office, and I could see a large note on my door. It read: "Nice job, you are our Sully. You made us proud!" This sign was being referenced from the pilot Captain Sully Sullenberger who landed his plane on the Hudson one month prior to this accident. He was the world's hero, and I was being told I was the same. I was so touched and humbled by their words.

A couple of weeks later, the town supervisor, Scott Bylewski, and I took all of my immediate staff out for a dinner that we paid for ourselves. We took fourteen or fifteen of our closest colleagues in this incident out for a nice steak dinner as a way to say thank you for all their hard work. It was a chance to unwind and sincerely thank each other. We joked around with some gag gifts, and I ended up receiving a Build-A-Bear—which is a teddy bear that you build with customizations and personal effects, usually for a child. These guys got together and made a Build-A-Bear of a fireman wearing the same reading glasses I used, my ID tag, and a replica of my famous yellow coat.

They were beating me up a little bit, kind of like a roast, but as strange as it sounds, that was great! It was an opportunity for Scott and me to thank these people who made our jobs possible, and at the same time, it was a chance to let our hair down and unwind. That was really helpful.

There were others, too, who helped me get through the aftermath. Father Joe, who was a friend of my family for forty-plus years, called me regularly, saying, "Hey, how are you doing, buddy? Anything you need?" Naturally, I would always respond, "No, I'm good." But his constant check was a lifeline. Knowing that he was there was so helpful. I wasn't asking for help, even though some might say, "You probably needed it." I might have, but I got through it in my own way. Is that the way we should conduct ourselves? Probably not. I'm an example of that. I got through it okay, but it was awkward and uneasy. I think what really helped me most were the requests for presentations that started coming in within about three or four weeks after the mission.

Thank God, I had the inspiration to put everything on a DVD before the emotion started to drain out of me. When I look back at that, I realize it was the right thing to do. I needed to capture that mood, and that became the starting point for a full-blown presentation. Being able to tell the story of the experience was one of my most effective coping mechanisms.

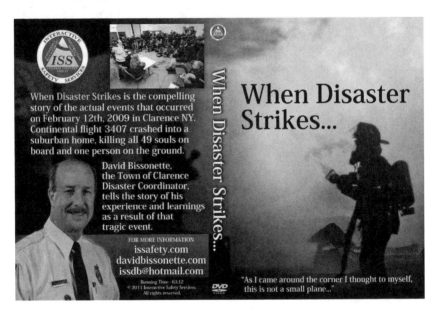

Most difficult to navigate for me, though, was the notoriety that went along with the operation. The thank-yous and appreciation, the questions from those desperate for answers—that was all very overwhelming to me. I think the public was searching for something or someone to key in on in with their appreciation, and because I was the face of the day-to-day update, that ended up being me. That wasn't a position I was looking to be in, but it was a default because of my involvement in the media. Whether I liked it or not, I would have to learn to accept my new identity and grow comfortable with my unlikely role as the face of a tragedy.

CHAPTER 9

ONE PERCENTER

Flight 3407 was rare. As of this writing, it and the Pilatus PC-12 crash in Montana, also in 2009, remain the last plane crashes with more than five casualties in the US.[1]

Flight 3407 was what we call a "one-percenter," meaning that out of all the emergency calls a first responder will receive, only about 1 percent of them will have a situation of such magnitude on the other end. They're incredibly rare—but when they do occur, you should hope your first responders are prepared to handle the devastation.

I learned a lot from 3407, from both a technical and a personal perspective. If I can help other first responders and emergency managers better prepare for the rarest of awful situations, then they're much better suited to respond to the most common varieties of bad situations. So let's look at some of the key learnings for responding to a one percenter.

---

1   "Recent US Plane Crashes," AirSafe, October 8, 2014, http://www.airsafe.com/events/us_ten.htm.

Emergency operations center. First and foremost, establish an EOC. Establishing a structure for command and control is critical to the success of any incident, particularly a major one. Think big. Assume that you will need one and a half to two times more than what you think you will. If you're thinking you need twenty offices and one large room, then find the capacity for forty offices and two large rooms. By building twice as big as you think you're going to need, you will leave yourself the capacity to flex up and down during the incident.

Know your limits. Be willing to recognize when you need help, and always speak up and ask for it when you do. So many emergency managers ask too late or not at all. That just leaves a bigger strain on resources that probably aren't capable of handling the volume in the first place. Your silence isn't helping anything or anyone; it only adds to the potential for failure or a less-than-acceptable outcome.

Communication. Communications are the Achilles heel to every emergency. Using the unified command approach puts a significant success factor in your communications. When representatives from each agency are present in your unified command operation, then they can talk directly to their own personnel in their own language. You cannot be an expert on everything, so let others do some of the talking where you can't.

Communications to the public is equally important. It has to be early and consistent so people can fall into rhythm with you. If reporters know there will be an update every day at a specific time, then they have less of a reason to be charging the scene or creating trouble for you elsewhere.

In the same vein as media relations, be sure that all press conferences are prebriefed. What I mean by that is everybody who's going to be a part of that press conference has a couple of items, maybe three or four bullet points, that they want to communicate and then sticks to the subjects they reviewed during the premedia briefing.

Having representatives from each agency with you is also a critical success factor in media relations. The questions about law enforcement should be answered by law enforcement. Questions about emergency services should be answered by emergency services. Local government questions should be answered by local government representatives. This is really important for a number of reasons. For one, it demonstrates that the incident is under a unified command, and that fosters public confidence. For another, sharing the responsibility also reduces performance pressure among all parties involved.

Span of control. The next big-ticket item, span of control, speaks to the idea of not trying to manage more subjects or tasks than you can properly focus on as a leader. I work with a three- to seven-task approach. Most emergency managers, and most first responders with some experience, can manage between two and five. The optimal task limit for me, and for most of us, is five. That means managing and taking responsibility for five tasks ranging in complexity and risk. That number can be flexed up or down based on complexity and risk. Also, make sure to appoint a person(s) to act on your behalf during absences.

Security. Addressing security immediately is also a key to success. There are two levels of security that need to be a focus very early on. There's immediate scene security for the site of the incident. That's a hard line of security that doesn't allow anyone except those with a business need to enter that area. The second area of security is more of a general net at a radius of maybe half a mile away, for example, to prevent unnecessary people from entering the area.

Credentials. If you don't have a credentialing process, that means you aren't properly vetting the people who approach your perimeter. And if you don't have a way to determine whether they belong there or not, then the security of your incident is doomed. You have to have a way to anticipate who is coming and verify that the people presenting credentials have, in fact, been requested and deployed to your incident. You have to have a way to confirm that before they enter your incident to do whatever it is they're there to do.

Social media. Social media has become one of the biggest and still-growing new subjects in first response, emergency management, and incident control. It's absolutely imperative to have a way to manage social media today. Media blackouts and professional commitments by first responders not to communicate their observations of their experience through Facebook, e-mail, YouTube, Twitter, Instagram, or any other social media tool are must-haves in today's world.

It's more of a professional courtesy—a professional conduct issue, if you will—but it's still something we need to continue to address with our agencies to keep the credibility of the first-response community intact. Much of the work in which we're involved isn't appropriate for everyone to see and hear, and we must respect that fact.

Economy. In the remediation phase, I mentioned the importance of being sensitive to local businesses while maintaining a reasonable secured perimeter. Try to be sensitive to the economy of the area by providing as much access as physically possible for the public in order to support small business. That's something that the economy will remember later after the incident passes. These are the people we serve, so always try to make sure you stay sensitive to the livelihoods and needs of the residents in a town.

Demonstrations. A national or global incident is an opportunity for various groups to seize the spotlight for their own specific gains. I had an experience with an extremist group from another state that traveled to our town to leverage that global spotlight for a crude and hateful antihomosexuality campaign. This type of thing is likely to happen. There are people who will use these types of events as opportunities to publicize their mission. You have to plan for that and have a strategy in mind should it occur so that you can keep it minimized and out of the public eye. This particular group ended up capturing very little press for itself, which was a testament to the cooperation I had with the media at the time. I specifically asked the anchors of the local news agencies not to carry the demonstrations, and the public never heard the story in the news that day because of those relationships I established early in the incident.

Mourning. Lastly, there needs to be a time to mourn for both the families of the deceased as well as the public who experience the event. Whether a community holds vigils, public memorial services, funerals, or any other events honoring the victims, you literally must schedule time in your incident for these things to occur. You need to allow time for the public to be on the scene, time for the families to reflect and grieve, and time for the public to express their sorrow and their loss. These are not typical things we put in our planning stages, but they are a crucial component of compassionate leadership.

RARELY *PUT* FIRST: THE STATE OF VOLUNTEER FIRST RESPONDERS

With the constant danger and a volunteer environment, I'm frequently asked why first responders do what we do at all. Obviously I can't speak for everyone, but for me, the answer isn't all that surprising, really. I simply can't remember ever wanting to do anything else. You might say it was in my blood, and the same can be said for most of my colleagues. We were second-, third-, and fourth-generation residents brought up in the tradition of community service and feeling the pride that comes from helping others. The money certainly wasn't a motivator, then or now, as most fire departments throughout the country are composed entirely of volunteers. You're clearly not going to generate a livelihood as a volunteer firefighter, so if you're looking for a life of your own, starting a family perhaps, how this occupation will fit into those goals can only be answered by the individual.

Whether it's fire, police, EMS, or any other type of public safety and emergency-services department, these are people who train year-round for very little acknowledgement or pay, putting their lives on the line day in and day out. Only rarely do you get to see them, but they're there all the time regardless.

Today, according to the National Fire Protection Association (NFPA), 69 percent of all US firefighters are volunteers.[2] That statistic alone speaks to the character of humankind, that we still have a significant segment of the population that's willing and capable of helping their fellow persons. But consider this as well: Until about ten years ago, there was no compensation at all for volunteer firefighters; training and education courses were expected to be paid for by the volunteer. (Even for those who are monetarily compensated today, the stipend is very low, sometimes as low as $1,000 per year.) There was no retirement program, no benefits, no incentives at all in those days, really. Sure, there's an adrenaline rush and personal satisfaction from getting involved in any kind of volunteer work, but at

2   Hylton Haynes and Gary Stein, "U.S. fire department profile," NFPA, January 2016, http://www.nfpa.org/news-and-research/fire-statistics-and-reports/fire-statistics/the-fire-service/administration/us-fire-department-profile.

the end of the day, you're putting your life in danger to protect your own community from what will or could happen. My dad introduced me to that side of the community-service world when he was the fire commissioner, and I've pledged my allegiance to it ever since.

My biggest fear, in terms of disaster preparation, is the declining state of volunteerism as communities expand or compress. When the chips are down, who are those communities counting on? With a typical volunteer service, the continuing erosion of volunteerism puts communities more and more at risk of a disaster without much relief. Had we not been prepared and funded to respond quickly and properly, who knows how much worse the 3407 tragedy could have been.

Throughout the Flight 3407 response, I think the public was introduced, in many ways, to this life we live. There was nothing else driving me, or any of us, except our work ethic, our concern for our fellow humans, and the quality of life for the residents in the area. I think people realized that and found trust in me—and, by extension, the rest of the first responder community—because I wasn't a politician and my conduct was the furthest kind from political. Anyone else who gets in front of the camera, you wonder what his or her ulterior motive is. Every one of these other agencies has promotional potential, but the emergency coordinator really has nowhere else to go, and that fact, I believe, builds more credibility and trust among the public.

In all, though, perhaps the best answer for why most of us do this kind of work is a fairly simple one: to make a difference for our neighbor. Most emergency responders I know would say, "That's the only reason I'm here. I just want to make things better than they would've been had I not been there." It should connect you to the community you serve, and that's the mission. In the end, that's the only goal we should have.

CHAPTER 10

LIFE AFTER DEATH

A year after 3407, I was nominated for Citizen of the Year by the Town of Clarence, which is considered a very prestigious award in Clarence—one that I was humbled in receiving. More than a few hundred people showed up for the annual function, and following dinner the town honored me with the award.

I was overwhelmed by the recognition, and I wrestled with how I could possibly accept the appreciation alone when so many others were also behind the mission's success. The recognition is not why you do these types of jobs. In fact, the rarity of recognition is what makes the work of first responders so sincere. To have the entire town recognizing me for our commitment to their quality of life was very satisfying, yet incredibly difficult to accept. These are people I've grown up with. I've lived in this town for forty-nine years, and a lot of the people at that dinner I'd known my whole life. They're family, and your family knows who you are—good, bad, or otherwise. To be recognized for the good, well, it's a night I'll never forget.

Along with that kind of recognition, however, comes a lot of guilt, at least for me. So when people began praising me personally, I felt uncomfortable, disingenuous somehow, as though the spotlight was pulling me away from my first-responder family.

That spilled over at home as well, and for about four or five years after the accident, there was some tension between Traci and I. We were grappling with how to absorb the event and where to put the experience in our lives. We talked about telling the story and making it a piece of my consulting business, but we struggled to agree on how we should do it. Traci has always been much more expressive than I am, and she was more comfortable with being public about telling our story and making a difference in other people's lives. In her mind, I had an opportunity to minimize some of the pain and agony people endure when going through this type of event, while I worried that I might be seen as trying to capitalize on a tragedy. She grew frustrated with me, saying to me finally, "When are you going to start accepting who you are and what you do and the value for that?" So how to tell the story without offending anyone involved became a very long conversation. On the surface, from the outside looking in, I would say we were on our way back to our normal life. But there was a continuing undertone of frustration for the two of us as to what to do with this experience, hence the reason we decided to write this book.

For the next two or three years after the crash, I was part of several more awards ceremonies. In my safety-professional world, I was recognized by the National Safety Council for their Courage and Leadership Award. That was a national recognition sponsored by some senior directors at General Mills who had put my name in the hat. That blew my mind, to realize that the home office in Minneapolis was so proud of the work I had done that they would sponsor me with a national organization. They even sent a delegate to Buffalo at the local National Safety Council convention here and presented it to me. That was just an incredibly nice thing to have happen—but the discomfort from being in the spotlight over a plane crash was still very much with me.

The town also took my yellow emergency-management coat from me at the end of the incident and framed it under glass in the town museum. The inscription on the window box, in so many words, says, "This coat, worn by Dave Bissonette, the emergency coordinator, symbolizes strength, control, and leadership throughout a traumatic time for our town."

That was priceless to me. To this day, it's humbling. I almost discounted a lot of that type

of feedback because, as you hear all the time from people in the limelight, I was just doing my job to the best of my ability. Nonetheless, the appreciation and acknowledgment felt really good.

A month or two after the crash, I had also received a letter from the Professional Firefighters Union of the City of Buffalo. The letter was written to, one, thank me for including them in the incident, and, two, to praise me for my professionalism on the job. I'll always keep that letter. Unionized, career firefighters recognizing a nonunion effort doesn't happen very often. They may think it—but they rarely put it in writing.

Let me be very clear—*I did none of this alone!* In all, there were 1,285 people who set foot on that crash site in the various stages of our response. On average, about seventy people were on the scene every single day, at all times. That number swelled to somewhere around 350 late in the first week, mostly from day three to day five. On those days, it felt like we had as many feet as square feet on the scene, and in fact we did on certain occasions. From the state troopers and the Ladies' Auxiliary that stood on that street corner for two weeks straight—with no complaints given, and no praise asked for—to the Clarence Center Fire Department, Chief Case, and the surrounding departments that found enough supernatural strength to fight for days the kind of inferno few will ever understand, to the community volunteers working overtime to lift the spirits of their fellow human beings—I remain at a loss for words when I think about them all. Most of them are people I've never actually met, despite having spent several days working round-the-clock on this tragedy alongside me.

I do know, however, that they were members of the fire service, HAZMAT, special operations, law enforcement, the ME's office, and mental-health support services. I know that there were remediation workers and known volunteers who were actually on the property or directly related to the operation. Altogether, we had a long list of organizations and agencies involved, without which we couldn't have been successful. That list includes thirteen volunteer fire departments; seven law-enforcement agencies; Buffalo airport officials; all three Erie County emergency-services departments; both the Erie County health and highway departments; the National Transportation Safety Board (NTSB); New York State Emergency Management Office (SEMO); the New York State Office of Fire Prevention and Control (OFPC); Twin City Ambulance; Buffalo Fire's Urban Search and Rescue (USAR) team; the Town of Clarence highway, engineering, and code-enforcement departments; the Red Cross; New York State Department of Environmental Conservation (DEC); and the New York State Health Department.

For years after the incident, I didn't talk much about my feelings. I probably internalize too much in general, as so many of us men do. I typically internalize the average accident so I don't bring it home. Traci didn't join the fire department. I did. But 3407 required me to talk more about the experiences my job has produced, and that's probably a fundamental failure for most first responders in their personal lives. That's a reason for this book, to have a parallel conversation relating the emotional and the tactical elements of a fatal disaster. My mental health, or my emotional perspective during the incident, was never easy to talk about, and that's a red flag for critical stress and the need for debriefing.

I had to give myself permission to unpack the incident in my mind before I could really make sense of what actually occurred, the magnitude of what we had all endured and still endure. I relived several moments when I was frustrated during the operation in order to find ways I could better handle similar moments in the future. It's not healthy to dwell on the past, but it's certainly irresponsible not to spend time reflecting on it.

Not everything went perfectly during those two weeks; not everything was done the way Dave Bissonette wanted it to be done. But I found comfort in knowing that there were far too many variables for me to be micromanaging every aspect of the operation. There's plenty to do in any major disaster, so anyone involved in leadership needs to make compromises where possible and move on to an area where he or she can make a difference.

There were things that occurred during this incident that I didn't want to see done—but they happened anyway. Were these deal-breakers for me? No. You have to put such things in their place and understand that the overall success or failure of an incident belongs to everyone. And that's something we have to keep reminding ourselves, that either we all fail or we all succeed. Regardless, we do it together.

In truth, my work as a consultant, traveling the country to share my experience and what I've learned throughout my career with others, may have been my saving grace after 3407. The decision to add another division to my consulting, specifically around emergency management, was directly related to my learnings from the 3407 air disaster and the call for information about the experience. I decided to tell the story from my perspective, with the feeling and compassion that was a part of our experience. If I could share my learnings and use the set of knowledge I gained to improve other first-response tactics, then I've done more with my career than I ever thought I could.

What has emerged since is beyond what I ever expected. I realize, too, just how much pride I have in Clarence and western New York. In 2014, a couple of other emergency managers and I were recognized nationally for best practices in planning for a hazardous materials incident and proactive planning for disasters. For me, that confirmed that we know what we're doing in this area, and I'm proud of that. There aren't too many incidents that we don't have a strategy for or resources to contribute. Not every town and county can say that, and I've never been prouder to be a part of this community and the fine people who dedicate their lives to looking after it.

For weeks after the crash, letters of gratitude, support, and acknowledgement poured into my mailbox. Many were from residents, some were from total strangers around the country, and some, the most overwhelming of them all, were from the families of victims. I still read some of those letters every once in a while, although I never seem to be able to read more than one or two at a time. It really makes you emotional to have people express their gratitude and grief to you, especially when they took the time to put it in writing and send it to you.

What has gotten me through this experience most was the realization that it wasn't really about me at all, not the awards, not the publicity, not the public appreciation, none of it. It wasn't about me—because I wasn't the only one people were seeing. People were recognizing the passion for serving and protecting our community that all public safety personnel hold—the sincerity of our efforts now on such wide display. I realized that I represented *all* those who do this kind of work, yet are so rarely acknowledged for it. I convinced myself that maybe through me—through this single event and all that came after it—they could have a voice and be heard. Today, I'm proud to tell my story. And in some small way, I hope that I'm telling all of theirs, too.

DAVID M. BISSONETTE

GLOSSARY OF FIELD TERMS

EM (Emergency Manager): the person tasked with public safety and large-scale incident-management planning and coordination under the authority of the town supervisor.

EOC (Emergency Operations Center): a designated location where all agency representatives meet to organize an operation for its entire duration.

ICS (Incident Command System): a predetermined organizational framework used for managing an incident.

NIMS (National Incident Management System): a standardized approach to incident management developed by the Department of Homeland Security; a systematic, proactive approach to guide departments and agencies at all levels of government, nongovernmental organizations, and the private sector to work together seamlessly and manage incidents involving all threats and hazards.

IC (Incident Commander): the person tasked with overall incident responsibility.

PIO (Public Information Officer): the person tasked with communicating accurate and consistent incident information to the public.

DEC (New York State Department of Environmental Conservation): state regulatory agency responsible for all aspects of environmental oversight.

NTSB (National Transportation Safety Board): federal agency responsible for investigation and root-cause analysis of all types of transportation disasters.

ME (Medical Examiner): a physician or other person trained in medicine to perform autopsies on the bodies of persons supposed to have died from unnatural causes and to investigate the causes and circumstances of such deaths.

FBI (Federal Bureau of Investigation): a national security and intelligence organization that protects and defends against terrorist and foreign intelligence threats.

HAZMAT (Hazard Materials Team): a specialized unit of fire service personal equipped and trained to manage hazardous materials spills and releases.

Unified Command: an assembled group of representatives from all agencies located at the EOC (Emergency Operations Center).

NFTA (Niagara Frontier Transportation Authority): an agency responsible for all airport and mass-transit operations in the Buffalo Niagara Region.

SEMO (New York State Emergency Management Office): an agency responsible for overall public safety and emergency planning for the residents of New York state.

OFPC (New York State Office of Fire Prevention and Control): agency responsible for fire prevention, training, and state standards.

USAR (Urban Search and Rescue): a specialized unit of fire-service personnel equipped and trained in confined space and building collapse rescue.